What People Are Saying About
Ready Set Start: Navigate Your Success

"Dynamic. Inspiring. Challenging. *Ready Set Start* hits the heart of the issue. Whether your vocation is minister, teacher, coach, motivational speaker, or simply someone who wants to know themselves better, this book is invaluable. As a leader of men for over 40 years, I speak from experience when I say, "If you don't know yourself, it is difficult to do any of those things or to help others. I only wish I'd have had this book 40 years ago; my life and job would have been so much easier."

Frank Bonvillain
Lieutenant Colonel, Infantry (Ret) U.S. Army

"Wendy lives what she teaches. *Ready Set Start* is transformational because Wendy has been where she takes you."

Nicholas Marks CEO, AIFC

"This book provides an easy-to-read roadmap that can take you from where you are to where you want to go. *Ready Set Start* ties together all the personal development - clearly laying out the steps you would have to take to achieve the success you've been wanting. The simplicity is what makes this so powerful. Embrace Wendy's tools in this book and create your future!"

Patsy Lim, FCA
CEO Equipped4Success

"Wendy Marman's *Ready Set Start* is a must-read page-turner. You will not want to put it down.
If you have ever felt alone, in a dark place, uncertain, insecure, insignificant, or not enough, then you need to read this book. *Ready Set Start* is full of wisdom from personal experience and extensive reading and research. Each chapter ends with a golden-nuggets summary. If your spirit has grown weary, yet deep within, there's a spark in you that stands ready

to reboot your life for greatness, this is the book for you!"
Dorothy Guy Bonvillain, Ph.D., CVO
Warrior Family Legacy Foundation.

"Wendy Marman has reminded us that we are all on a journey. Each one of us is trying to find the right path to follow. In *Ready Set Start*, Wendy gives us the secrets to following that light within each of us and getting started on life's great adventure! Thank you, Wendy, for providing us with this important toolset to help us reach our destination!"
Robert A. Rohm, Ph.D.
President Personality Insights

"Wendy shares how to embrace our life journey as an adventure waiting to be discovered. It is often said that in life, the mess in your message is your mission if you so choose to accept it. I frequently asked myself, "Why am I here?" However, after reading *Ready Set Start*, I found that the better question to ask myself is, "Who am I here for, and how do I get started?"
JJ Brun, The Retired Spy

"Inspired! That is what *Ready Set Start* made me feel. Wendy takes you on a journey through your beliefs and shows you a pathway to design your own life, the life you want and crave. I particularly enjoyed the brief exercises that followed each chapter. So, if you are looking for more in life, look no further. *Ready Set Start* is the book we have all been waiting for."
Joanne Rutter Holbrook,
International Speaker and Author of *Passport to Parenting*

"*Ready Set Start* is filled with personal stories, quotes, and advice on how to dig in on life; this book will help you think of new thoughts and guide new actions. Thank you, Wendy, for stepping up to share your story and encourage us all."
Morgan Hendrix, Owner of Wild + Brave

"If you are weary, lonely, struggling with any area of your life, or just plain restless, this book is for you. The author guides you on a journey, with

gentle wisdom and understanding, gained from a life well-lived. This book is filled with life-changing stories and easy-to-apply, practical principles sprinkled with thought-provoking questions. If you answer the questions and apply the principles, this book will change your life forever."
Amanda Heal, Inspirational Speaker
Author of *Seeing by Vision Not by Sight: How to Discover Your Life's Purpose and Put It into Action*

"Knowing that life is a journey full of mountains to be climbed and not a final destination to arrive at. In this book, Wendy Marman guides you to what is possible in your life when you commit to getting started on the path of achieving what is possible for your future. Get ready to stretch your mind and heart to make the rest of your life the best of your life!"
Patrick Snow, Publishing Coaching and International Best-Selling Author of *Creating Your Own Destiny*

"Wendy mentored me to find my passion and how to start and follow my dream. Wendy and her *Ready Set Start* program have truly changed my life and my family's life."
Paulette Thacker, CEO Pro-Com Services

READY
SET
START

Navigating Your Success

Written by
Wendy Marman
www.wendymarman.com

Skinny Brown Dog Media
www.SkinnyBrownDogMedia.com

Copyright © 2022 Wendy Marman
http//WendyMarman.com

All rights reserved

This publication is designed to provide accurate and authoritative information in regard to the subject matter covered. It is sold with the understanding that publisher and author are not engaged in rendering legal, accounting, medical or other professional services. Nothing herein shall create a client relationship, and nothing herein shall constitute legal, medical, professional advice. If legal, medical, or other professional services or advice is required, a competent professional should be sought.

Published by Skinny Brown Dog Media
Atlanta, Punta del Este
http//www.skinnybrowndogmedia.com

Distributed by Skinny Brown Dog Media
Developmental Editing and Design by Eric G. Reid
Cover Design by Skinny Brown Dog Media

Publisher's Cataloging-in-Publication Data

Print ISBN 978-1-957-506-00-5
eBook ISBN 978-1-957-506-01-2
Hardback ISBN 978-1-957-506-02-9
Library of Congress Control Number 2022901080

Ready Set Start may be purchased in bulk for educational, business, fundraising. For information, please email Wendy@WendyMarman.com

DEDICATION

To my mother, Rosalind Shearer, MB.BS. (Syd), FRCS (Edin), (1928-2012) You believed in me, and your belief was steadfast and infectious in the best possible way. You role modeled courage, commitment, love, and family. You encouraged me to create and live my adventure, go after my dreams, and become all I could be. I miss you. Thank you with all my heart.

To my husband, Patrick Marman, and my children, Hugh, Anna, Rosalie, and Heather, I love that you are following your own gifting and dreams. With your families, you are now creating your own adventures. I love you. I am proud of you. You inspire me daily. Because of you, the adventure continues.

Table of Contents

Starting Where You Are	3
Walking In Hope	14
Navigating The Darkness	25
Journeying in the Light	38
Knowing and Loving You	49
Building Your Strength	63
Feeding Your Tomorrows	71
Measuring and Tracking Your Progress	79
Connecting with Your World	91
Navigating Your Life	102
Harnessing the Power of Persistence	111
Releasing Your Power Through Habits	125
Being Resilient	137
Showing the Way	151
Continuing Your Adventure	157

*"The only impossible journey
is the one
you never begin."*

Tony Robbins

READY

Chapter 1
Starting Where You Are

"It's not the mountain we conquer but ourselves."
Sir Edmund Hillary

Life is a journey. Adventure is a choice.

It was two in the morning. It was dark, and it was cold. Stars twinkled in a black inky sky. I stood outside a hut at 11,000 feet above sea level near the summit of Mount Kinabalu in Borneo, Malaysia. In my hands, I held a bottle of water, some food, and a flashlight as I prepared for the journey ahead. Despite being in the tropics, it was cold standing there in my black merino wool leggings, a beanie, gloves, and a polar fleece jacket. Our small group, dressed in an assortment of clothing designed for functionality rather than style, stood with me, looking sleepy and somewhat shellshocked. Muted groaning filled the air as our limbs, still sore from the climb we had completed the day before, protested the idea of an early morning climb.

This morning's climb would be a journey of choice and will. None of us had to be there. No reward or prize was offered for what we were about to do, other than the experience. We had chosen to be there, and despite our moans, we each woke at the crack of dawn. That morning, we had two guides—one to lead and one to pull up the rear. Our goal that day was to get up before dawn and reach the mountain peak in time to experience the sunrise at 13,435 feet. Sleepy, aching, and uncertain, our little group started to climb through the darkness.

I was the slowest of our group. I think the guides worried if I would make it to the summit. As I struggled to climb in the dark, I also wondered if I would complete the climb. I slowly crept my way up the mountainside. Together, we climbed, walked, and scrambled over the rocks. We used ladders and ropes to ascend small cliff faces in the dark. As the climb got steeper, I moved slower. My breathing was labored. I would take a few steps, pause, moan, step, climb, stumble, pause, repeat. That was my pace. I am sure the guide thought I sounded like I would die while the group continued to stretch out ahead of me.

Towards the summit, the climb leveled out. With one final push needed to reach the peak, I increased my pace as I crossed over a somewhat open, flat, rocky area. Climbing was easier on the flatter terrain, despite the altitude. I was the straggler of the group, but I was persistent. I kept putting one foot in front of the other. Knowing the sunrise was fast approaching, I started to move even faster. Then, just as the sun broke the horizon, I reached the top. Standing there, seeing the sky ignite into a new day, took my breath away. That single moment between dawn and daybreak was so worth it! It didn't matter that I wasn't the first to arrive. It didn't matter that I struggled on the way up. As the sun greeted me on the summit, the beauty and wonder of that moment are with me still. I will cherish that experience forever.

EXERCISE

1. What adversity or mountains have you climbed to get where you are today?

_____

_____

_____

_____

ARE YOU READY FOR THE NEXT CLIMB TO YOUR SUMMIT?

When I started climbing to the summit, I wasn't sure if I could make it. I knew I could walk the distance on flat land, and I knew I was persistent, but it was a long, long way—almost straight up. Altitude sickness was a real possibility, and I was one of the oldest in our group. This climb was something I hadn't done before, and I had no experience climbing mountains.

So, every step of the climb would literally be a first. My mountain journey was more than a physical journey. It was a journey in self-leadership. I held on to a promise I had made to myself to do my best and not give up. At some points on the climb, sheer obstinance and willpower allowed me to lift my leg and take the next step. As Sir Edmund Hilary said, "I didn't conquer the mountain. I conquered myself."

You may feel unsure or hesitant as you begin your journey to your success. Be encouraged. That's normal, and it doesn't have to stop you from starting the journey. Make yourself a promise to persist, to keep moving forward regardless of the pace. Persistence is a powerful force in creating change.

The trip to Mount Kinabalu in Borneo, Malaysia, in 2007 is now a fantastic memory and an inspiration for me. I now know, "I can climb mountains." When feeling doubtful, I tell myself, "Remember Mount Kinabalu," and my doubt is challenged by hope. "Maybe I can. What if I can! It is worth the journey. It is worth the try!" Hope then births possibility. I ask, "How can I?" Possibility empowers action. Step by step, a new journey begins. Life becomes an adventure!

EXERCISE

What mountains stand in your way right now?

_____

_____

_____

_____

What possibilities do you see for your life if you could start to conquer that mountain?

_____

_____

_____

_____

STARTING WHERE YOU ARE

One of my favorite old Irish sayings is, "Ah, if I were going there, I wouldn't start from here." It recognizes that we often don't want to be where we are when we decide to start something. Sometimes we wish we were somewhere else. It also acknowledges that not all starting points are equal. You may not like where you are; you may wish you were at a different starting point, but don't let that stop you! Some journeys begin in darkness, physically as mine did on Mount Kinabalu, or figuratively. Others begin in the light of day, but that doesn't matter either way. You start from wherever you are.

STARTING FROM LOST

I felt lost and totally frustrated, working a job that was killing me—or so it felt. Then through an unexpected mentor, I found hope.

My journey from lost started one day while driving down the main street of Melbourne, Australia. A name from my childhood appeared before me. I couldn't believe it. My unexpected mentor's name flapped before my eyes on dozens of colorful flags promoting a live theatre production.

I had first seen my unexpected mentor when I was a child. My mother took me to the cinema to see *Bedknobs and Broomsticks*, where my unexpected mentor played the leading role. Years later, my family and I would be snuggled on the couch together watching her, as Jessica Fletcher, solve crimes in Cabot Cove, Maine. Yes, my unexpected mentor was Irish American actor Angela Lansbury.

When I saw her name on those flapping flags, my first thought was, *It must be someone else. The Angela Lansbury I know and love must be one hundred by now!* In disbelief, I went home and looked up the stage production only to find out it was the same Angela Lansbury, and no, she wasn't one hundred. She was eighty-nine and acting the title role in *Driving Miss Daisy*. I thought, *Eighty-nine, someone must be paying her well to come to Australia, to do what she loves and excels in doing—a role that brings joy to many.*

The idea that someone could pay me at eighty-nine to do what I love and am good at got me thinking. Angela Lansbury had shown me what was possible. She made my excuses for not getting started on the next adventure of my life seem lame. Her example birthed my desire to go for my dream regardless of my age. I started asking myself what would need to happen to make the changes I needed to make. Once I started asking myself possibility-based questions, it was like flicking on a light switch. I came alive. Angela Lansbury helped me turn on my light within and my desire to start. I could see hope and possibilities where previously there was only frustration and darkness.

I have not met Ms. Lansbury personally yet. But, when I do, I will tell her how thankful I am that she came into my life and showed me what was possible. Simply by living her life, by being herself, Angela Lansbury set an example and changed my life forever. She is now part of my story.

Today, you may only have a glimpse of the possibilities for a better future. But know, from just those glimpses, it is enough to start. You can navigate your success journey no matter where you are and what you see.

My journey to success has become an exciting adventure that I could not have imagined when I started. This journey has impacted not only my life but the lives of all around me, especially those I care for most deeply. At times it has been more complicated than I expected. I am thankful for a mentor who gave me the gift of hope and helped me find direction when I was lost. By being you and living your best life possible, you can become an inspiration for others. You might just become someone's unexpected accidental mentor, too.

The path for me wasn't straight or fast. Neither will yours be, but after all, it is an adventure, and that's what makes it exciting. My journey began by learning to know myself and lead myself in a whole new way. You will start the same way. After all, we are the only ones who can lead ourselves to the next level of success. Mentors and guides can encourage and inspire us, but we must take the first step. That first step starts with our thinking. When I learned to lead myself, I knew I had discovered the foundation of a life of success.

To lead me and move forward, I knew I first had to face who I was and where I was in my life, then agree that was the starting point.

How do you figure out where you are?

How you answer the questions below will become your basecamp, your starting point. You may not think your starting point is ideal, but it's perfect for you! Knowing where you really are and writing it down will help you get started, track your progress, and better see your path ahead. In addition, the clarity gained from being honest about where you are now will help you set priorities and plan your course of action to create your new future.

EXERCISE

A quick basecamp check-in

1. My current daily concern is focused on
   - ☐ A. "Will I survive?"
   - ☐ B. "Will I be accepted?"
   - ☐ C. "Am I living my truth, growing into my potential, and inspiring others?"

2. Most of my energy is spent on
   - ☐ A. Safety
   - ☐ B. Security
   - ☐ C. Freedom

3. Obstacles and problems often lead me to
   - ☐ A. Stop
   - ☐ B. Get Stuck
   - ☐ C. Learn and Lean in

4. I often feel _____ when I think about the next three years of my life.
   - ☐ A. Trapped, Fearful
   - ☐ B. Bored, Frustrated
   - ☐ C. Free, Energized

The more A boxes you checked, the more you are living an unfulfilled life.
The more B boxes you checked, the more you are living a settled life.
The more C boxes you checked, the more you are living success on your terms.

Now that you have gained clarity, you don't have to wait for a specific set of circumstances to start to change.

LEARNING TO DEFINE SUCCESS ON YOUR TERMS

Success is not your success unless it includes what is most important to you! Success is often defined by material acquisitions or financial wealth. For some, the idea of achieving success is a loaded word, full of judgment, or something other people can be or do! Success and what it means has to be about what is essential for you.

As you map out your success, you will be asked to challenge your current beliefs and thinking. When you challenge your beliefs, you will also face your fears. Facing your fears, you will define your success to include what is most important to you. As a result, your success will fit you perfectly and be something you are and can live every day!

EXERCISE

Name one fear or belief that is holding you back.

_____

_____

_____

_____

START WITH HOPE

Sometimes you start your journey with nothing more than hope. When I stood at the bottom of Mount Kinabalu, my mind raced through thoughts of "What have I done?" and "What have I gotten myself into?" Before starting Mount Kinabalu, I had to get my mind, attitude, and self-talk working for me instead of against me. When I started that climb, all I had was hope. With each step, the hope grew into confidence. I was at the same point when I decided to define success on my terms.

Whether you feel you are facing huge mountains or just wishing to make a few gentle changes, the strategies in this book will be your guideposts. Start with hope and take the steps provided. Define success on your terms, and step by step, you will learn the skills to navigate your success and live it every day.

REMOVING EXCUSES

To move forward will require overcoming the roadblocks. For example, when reading *The Magic of Thinking Big* by David J. Schwartz, I was confronted with two life-changing ideas. The first was that *excusitis* is a dangerous disease that takes various forms:

- Age *excusitis* - I'm too old; I'm too young.
- Gender *excusitis* - Only women/men can do that.
- Education *excusitis* - I'm not smart enough; I don't have the qualifications.

You get the point. I had to face the truth that what I had called my "logical reasons" for not starting were excuses or *exusitis*. And that *exusitis* was robbing me of my dreams. To move to the next level, I needed to break the power of *excusitis* in my life and redefine my success journey.

The second idea I learned from *The Magic of Thinking Big* that changed my life was "Action Cures Fear." Any action. The action you take doesn't have to be perfect or grand. Simple, small action will break down fear.

EXERCISE

1. Can you think of a time that maybe excusitis held you back?-

_____

_____

_____

_____

_____

2. What small action can you take now to break through that excuse?

_____

_____

_____

_____

START BECOMING INSPIRED

Inspiration is a power source to help you break through some of the toughest excuses. For me, listening to and learning other people's stories inspires me. Hearing other people's stories helps me face my excuses and act. If I want to do something that I have not done before, I find someone who has walked a similar path and learn all I can from them. Then, I use their success to inspire me to start. Cliff Young, an ultra-marathoner, is one person who inspired me to break through my self-limiting thinking and doubts.

Cliff Young was a sheep farmer who started running in events when he was 57. At 61-years-old Cliff won the inaugural Sydney to Melbourne Ultramarathon, a distance of 875 kilometers (544 mi). The fun part of the story is that Cliff competed in his overalls and gumboots without his dentures because he said they rattled when he ran. Cliff started where he was, with what he had. He ran slowly and trailed the pack by a considerable distance at the end of the first day. Did he give up? No, he just kept doing what he knew worked for him. He ran his race. While the other competitors stopped to sleep for six hours, Young kept running, only stopping to sleep two hours. After the first night, Cliff took the lead. At the end of the race, he won by a lead of ten hours. Cliff completed the course in five days, fifteen hours, and four minutes—almost two days faster than the previous record. Cliff Young was asked what helped him stay on the course. He said that during the race, he imagined he was running after sheep, trying to outrun a storm.

Cliff Young's story inspired me to face my age excusitis and get started.

FACE YOUR FEARS

Another person's story that inspired me is a professional colleague, Amanda Heal. Amanda refuses to let her blindness be an excuse. Amanda attended public schools and went to a university, earning her law degree. Then she worked for many years in government before starting her own business and writing her first book. Amanda has now completed her second book, *Seeing by Vision, Not by Sight*. Amanda may be blind, but her vision is profound. Most remarkable to me was watching her when she traveled internationally to a leadership training event. Seeing how she navigated the huge crowds and crowded hotel spaces in pursuit of her dream humbled me sometimes.

One of the most profound lessons I learned from Amanda came from her answer to a question I asked her about the greatest fear she had overcome. "My greatest fear," said Amanda, "was learning to catch a bus." Something so practical and so personal. I and everyone in the room that day learned just how very personal our fears are to each of us. When you are blind, like Amanda, something as simple as catching a bus can hold you in deep fear.

The fear holding you back may seem simple, but it is your fear, and that feeling may be intense. Know that you can face your fear, face your feelings, and achieve the breakthrough you need to get started. Today, Amanda and her guide dog, Sadie, regularly train new bus drivers on how to assist blind people and their guide dogs.

ALWAYS CHOOSING ADVENTURE

Adventure is always a choice. There is one truth for all journeys; you will face challenges. Things will go wrong. You will fall as you move forward. That is the adventure of being a human in growth. Staying where you are to avoid problems is false security. Embracing the possibilities of falling and failing is, in fact, the only way you can progress and create your success.

Have you ever noticed how fear and excitement are similar feelings?

All journeys start with a mixture of fear and excitement. Then, you make the choice of which to follow.

You are leading you! Are you willing to lead yourself to something new starting today? Are you willing to lead your life, step by step, moment by moment, regardless of the fear? Are you willing to choose excitement over fear? The choice is yours.

SUMMARY

- Life is a journey. Adventure is an option.
- Start where you are.
- You may start in darkness; start anyway.
- Your journey will not be easy but so worth the risk!
- To start:
    1. Start with hope.
    2. Face your fears and excuses.
    3. Surround yourself with people who can help and inspire you.
    4. Lead yourself.

Chapter 2
Walking In Hope

"Hope is the pillar that holds up the world."
Pliny the Elder

In chapter one, I shared that life is like a journey up a mountain, a journey you can start with hope. Now I want to share a little more about the power of hope to get you started.

The thing I love is that hope is both a noun and a verb. Hope is something you have and something you do. Hope includes a feeling of expectation, wanting something to happen, and believing something good may happen.

You don't hope for something you already have! You hope for something you want to experience. Hope, by definition, exists in the unseen. Why then is hope so important to us? Because hope is the power behind all change and growth. With all that is happening in the world, the idea of starting with hope may seem too elusive, impractical, and naive. I disagree. Hope is real, effective, and powerful. Hope is the thing that gets you started and leads you forward. Like a muscle, hope can grow stronger every time you use it. Hope in action is the creative power for your life.

When I worked for the government, I often heard the saying, "Hope is not a strategy." Perhaps you have heard it, too. I agree that hope is not a strategy for project management nor a replacement for good planning, but accepting that hope is one of the most potent forces in the universe is a great strategy to get started. Without hope, you will not take the first step. With hope, you will begin to persevere when all things seem impossible. With hope as part of your strategy, you will break through seemingly impossible odds. Hope also buys you time to build your strength, discover your purpose, and create your future. Your success builds through hope and purpose to move into the future.

EXERCISE

1. What are the hopes of your heart?

_____

_____

_____

_____

Hope also drives action. They said it was impossible to break the four-minute mile! But, fueled by hope, Roger Bannister proved them wrong in Oxford, England, on May 6, 1954. Seven men were entered in that one-mile race. Bannister entered the race with one additional element—hope. In his heart, he knew he was prepared and ready to win that day. What he hoped for was something more significant than a win. The stadium announcer teased the crowd by delaying his announcement of Bannister's winning time for as long as possible. He then calmly announced:

"Ladies and gentlemen, here is the result of event nine, the one-mile first, number forty-one, R.G. Bannister, Amateur Athletic Association and formerly of Exeter and Merton Colleges, Oxford, with a time which is a new meeting and track record, and which subject to ratification will be a new English Native, British National, All-Comers, European, British Empire, and World Record. The time was three..."

The roar of the crowd drowned out the rest of the announcement. Bannister's time was 3 minutes, 59.4 seconds. The "impossible" had been achieved; the four-minute mile was broken. Forty-six days later, Bannister's record was broken by his rival, John Landy. Before, Bannister breaking the four-minute mile seemed like something that could never be achieved. But, after Roger Bannister showed it could be done, more and more athletes ran the mile in under four minutes from that day on. Today, all top one-mile runners break that barrier. Bannister blazed the trail for them, built on his hope of being the first.

Does the challenge you currently face feel impossible? Every idea and strategy in this book comes from someone who has gone before you and shows you the impossible is possible. The stories and people are here to lead the way!

STEPPING FORWARD

Roger Bannister could have given up after he tried to break the four-minute barrier the week before under ideal conditions. At the 1952 Olympics, Roger Bannister finished fourth. After this "relative failure", Bannister spent the next two months deciding whether to give up running altogether. Coming close to the four-minute mile made Bannister realize that setting a sub-four-minute mile time was not out of reach for someone. But would it be him that showed the world the full possibilities? That was his struggle.

Bannister set a goal to be the first to run a mile in under four minutes. He committed himself to this goal and worked even harder. The hope of achieving this goal led to his commitment to see it through to the end. That commitment led to the actions he needed to take daily to be ready for the opportunity.

To achieve success, you have to be ready for learning, failing, learning, trying again and again until hope is fulfilled.

What are you willing to commit to? Will you learn from your failures and keep going? Will you commit to learning, growing, and improving your actions until you achieve success as you define it?

EXERCISE

1. Write your commitment statement for the journey ahead. Start with the statement, "I commit to…"

_____

_____

_____

_____

2. "I will take the following action…"

_____

_____

_____

_____

Remember, even if you are unsure of precisely all the action steps you need to take, you can start to achieve your goal with what you know now. Action has a way of creating clarity and revealing the next action. Action often begins in the mind, shifting your thinking from impossible to possible. It may seem small, but it is a substantial action for many.

Here are four things I tell myself to help me get started to take action:
1. Hope is my superpower. It gets me started and keeps me going.
2. I can learn what I need to know along the way.
3. All action, big or small, is worth it.
4. I choose to take responsibility and lead myself.

EXERCISE

It is easy to create Get Started prompts to encourage you with modern technology.

Create a few Get Started reminders, then post them on your phone's screensaver, on sticky notes around your computer, place a printed card in your wallet, or post reminders around the house. Get Started prompts are statements that start with "I can," "I will," or "I am."

     a. I can do it.
     b. I can learn anything I need.
     c. It is always worth it.
     d. I will go step by step.
     e. I have hope.
     f. I will find a way.
     g. I will persist.
     h. I will learn today and be better tomorrow.

When I started my journey towards my new success, I seemed to have more questions than answers. I didn't know what to do or how to begin rebuilding my life. I knew I had to do something different from what I had been doing, and I hoped to figure out how to make it all work along the journey. The hope I had for a better life lit a light within me. That inner light has guided me through many challenges and dark times. Through all the struggle and uncertainty, my hope could not be extinguished. I fed that hope. As I grew my confidence and knowledge, my world expanded, new horizons opened up, and my uncertain journey became filled with adventure instead of fear.

I call it a journey because it is a trip from one place to another, usually taking a relatively long time. Journey also means to progress from one stage to another. For example, your journey to success is about moving from one level to the next, then the next. A Journey can also be something you do.

Your journey will always:
- Start wherever you are.
- Take time. In fact, it could take a lifetime.
- Require you to take action to make it happen.
- Require you to grow and change.
- Cost you more than you expect.
- Reward you with more than you could dream.

Your journey will require you to embrace the reality of your current situation. Where you are now is the result of your choices and actions you took (or did not take) to lead you to this point. When you acknowledge your reality, you can fully embrace your journey.

In 1923 Viktor Frankl, a young Jewish man from Vienna, Austria, started medical school. He would go on to specialize in neurology and psychiatry. In 1926, Dr. Frankl began refining his idea that meaning was the central motivational force in human beings—that a sense of meaning gave humanity a sense of purpose.

Nazi's annexation of Austria changed everything for the Jewish community and Dr. Frankl and his wife, Tilly. Doctor and Mrs. Frankl were sent to Nazi concentration camps along with many of their fellow Jewish colleagues. Tilly died shortly after.
Despite all that he suffered, Dr. Viktor Frankl survived years in a concentration camp, finally being released at the war's end. When Frankl returned to Vienna, he wrote *Man's Search for Meaning*, a small booklet documenting the events and lessons learned from his concentration camp experience.

Today, *Man's Search for Meaning* is still recognized as one of the most influential essays on humanity and the search for purpose in life. The wisdom in *Man's Search for Meaning* has been one of the most powerfully positive influences in my life.

Dr. Frankl's personal story in *Man's Search for Meaning* teaches us how to embrace even the most horrendous parts of any journey. And how in embracing the bad, we can better understand and connect to our desire to achieve something big, bold, and sound. The wisdom and compassion Dr. Frankl showed in his book provided me much-needed light in my life to face and move through some of the most challenging and darkest passages of my own life.

Two of the biggest lessons that stood out for me from *Man's Search for Meaning* are:

1. True Freedom.

Dr. Frankl put it this way… *"The last of the human freedoms is to choose one's attitude in any given set of circumstances, to choose one's own way."*

Dr. Frankl explains, "And there were always choices to make [in the concentration camp]. Every day, every hour, offered the opportunity to make a decision, a decision which determined whether you would or would not submit to those powers which threatened to rob you of your very self, your inner freedom; which determined whether or not you would become the plaything to circumstance, renouncing freedom and dignity…"

"Even where there seemed to be no choice, I had a choice. In that choice was my freedom."

Wow! That one idea—having a choice has freedom—has changed my life in so many ways.

2. The Power of Why

Dr. Frankl quotes Nietzsche when explaining his time in the concentration camp: "Those who have a 'why' to live, can bear with almost any 'how.'"

Dr. Frankl's story opened my eyes to the power of knowing my why. His story sent me on a journey to find my own "why" — a why big enough to compel me through anything. When I found my why, I found meaning, I found my power, and I found my way through.

I don't know what you are going through or will go through, but I do know two things:

1. You can do it.
   You can go through even the darkest moments and come out the other side.
2. It is worth it, and you are worth it.
   Your "why" is worth it. The journey through is always worth it.

EXERCISE

1. Where do you need to exercise your freedom and choose a new attitude?

   _____
   _____
   _____
   _____

2. What is your "why"?

   _____
   _____
   _____
   _____

The journey you are taking is not only external, but you face the challenges your life throws at you. Your journey starts internally. All real change starts first in the mind. It is the mind that hopes and determines that first action.

You may have heard the saying, "If you keep doing the same thing, you will keep getting the same results." What you may not have understood is it could also be written, "If you keep thinking the same things, you will keep getting the same results."

Have you ever thought, "There has got to be more to life than this?"

EXERCISE

Pause here for a moment and think about these things:

- Did you matter today?
- Did you take an action-based understanding that you were creating something better?
- What thoughts would you need to change to take better action tomorrow?

I haven't always been a hopeful person. Several years ago, I felt frustrated and lost. *How could I be here?* I'd done my best. I'd fulfilled my responsibilities. I had a family that I loved, and they loved me. I had a good job and volunteered in my community. Yet, why didn't I feel happy and fulfilled? Why did I think that somehow, without noticing it, I had lost control of my life and was now just going through the motions? Surely there was more to life than this, right? The hope in my heart answered, "Yes, there is more to life than you are experiencing."

Asking myself the question "there has to be more" was the beginning of the journey to take back my life. I didn't know what I would do next, nor how. All I knew was that I had to grow and change for my life to grow and change, so that's what I did. I started growing. I started to challenge and change my thinking, attitude, and actions. I added knowledge skills and developed the strengths needed for the new me. To do all this required courage, resilience, and the belief that it was possible.

Today, I have joy, energy, and health. Fantastic opportunities open before me that require me to continue stretching, learning, and growing. I know my life is worth living. More importantly, I know that living a life that matters is available to me and anyone else who chooses it.

I ask you questions about your life because reflecting on the current situation is the starting point. How you feel when you answer the questions is an indicator of the quality of your life. Your success moving forward will not be built on the "big" things or events that happen to you from time to time, nor your good intentions. Instead, your success will be built by making every day a success. Let me repeat that with a twist. Your success is built by making every day a success! It starts in you with hope. It begins with expanding your thinking.

The first settlement by Europeans in Australia was at Sydney Cove on January 26, 1788. Over the next few years, more ships came, more convicts and free settlers arrived. Conditions were hard. More food was needed to support the growing population, so the search for better land for agriculture and pastures led to pushing west. Suitable land was found at the foot of the Blue Mountains, but soon, even that was not enough. More land was needed, but the mountains blocked the way. Many tried to find passed mountains but came face to face with massive cliffs hundreds of feet high. It seemed there was no way through the mountains and unto open land. 1812 and 1813 brought severe droughts. Finding more farming land became even more urgent, but the settlers continued to do as they had always done to find a way past the mountains, and they continually failed.

Early in 1813, three men decided to do something different. This time, they would follow the mountain ridges, not the valleys. This plan went against all known wisdom, but the explorers hoped and acted differently. Finally, they found a way to cross the Blue Mountains. In July 1814, William Cox, my great, great, great grandfather, was commissioned to construct a road following the path the explorers discovered.

When I think of mountains, I think of my ancestors and the lesson that their thinking had to change before their actions could create a different result and the mountain could be conquered. Different thinking, different actions, different results. To achieve your success, you will need to embrace new thinking.

EXERCISE

1. Where would you like different results in your life?

_____

_____

_____

2. What old thinking would you need to challenge to change the results in your life?

_____

_____

_____

_____

Don't wait till things are desperate before you change. In his book, *The Fellowship of the Ring*, world-renowned author J.R.R. Tolkien shared how to embrace your journey in a beautiful way:

> *"Now far ahead the Road has gone,*
> *And I must follow, if I can,*
> *Pursuing it with eager feet."*

Eager feet! I love that expression. It is a great way to describe a life fueled with hope. Do you have eager feet for your life? For your adventure? For every day?

EXERCISE

1. Think about your life. Where are you dragging your feet? Why?

_____

_____

_____

_____

2. What would you need to change in your life to move with eager feet?

_____

_____

_____

_____

SUMMARY

- Hope in action is a creative power for life.
- When you know there is more to life, you are ready to start.
- Hope is about what you cannot yet see.
- Hope is powerful. Without it, you will do nothing.
- There will always be the decision to give up or keep going.
- To take control of your life, take control of yourself.
- You can learn what you need to know.
- Your journey is worth it.
- Hope strengthened leads to decision and commitment.
- Commitment leads to action and success.
- Your journey is an adventure that includes the good, the bad, and the ugly.
- You choose how you respond to what happens to you.
- When your "why" is big enough, you will find a way.
- Your thinking determines your actions, which determines your results.
- Be open to new thinking.
- Embrace your journey with eager feet.

Chapter 3
Navigating The Darkness

"I will love the light for it shows me the way, yet I will endure the darkness because it shows me the stars."
Og Mandino

We have all experienced moments of darkness in our life. Struggles or dark moments are all part of being human. This darkness becomes a problem when you cannot find your way forward or feel the darkness will never end. One of the secrets of success is being prepared for the struggles you will face on the road ahead.

Darkness is the partial or total absence of light. A room can be in darkness, so can your spirit, so can your life. A second meaning of darkness is wickedness or evil. When you feel the darkness in your life, it may be because you cannot see a solution at hand or because you have experienced wickedness or acts of evil—disappointment, loneliness, loss, trauma, abuse, or something else. Whether the darkness built up slowly or happened in a traumatic instant, you can start today and navigate through and out.

I want to provide you with the guideposts derived from my actual experiences of darkness and hope. If the darkness in your life has you feeling you are barely surviving, these guideposts will help you navigate from the darkness and despair, through hope, and into creating your new future, where you not only survive but thrive. The lessons in this chapter can be used whenever your path becomes unclear or you experience darkness.

New pilots learn early in their flight training how to deal with potential problems before they experience them. To fly at night, specialized instrument flying lessons are required to help you navigate when you cannot see landmarks below. Part of the goal of this chapter is to equip you to "fly by your own instruments" and chart your landmarks.

I don't know your exact story. But I know that whatever the reason you entered the darkness, you can navigate through it and come out the other side. No experience of darkness excludes you from creating the success you seek. Your past does not have to define your future, but your history can provide the reason and power to change!

A word of caution and a disclaimer before you move on.
As you reflect on the darkness in your life, it may trigger strong memories and pain. If this is true for you, and you feel unsafe, be courageous. Take a time out and seek the professional help you need. Your safety is the most important lesson.

I speak from the position of a coach, a guide, and a fellow traveler on this journey called life, not a medical doctor, psychologist, or counselor. This book is designed as food for hope and courage. Hope and courage are what it takes to face the darkness. It is not treatment; it is nourishment. Seeking help is not a weakness.

The first guidepost is about standing together, not taking the journey on your own.
Guidepost number two is about facing the current reality of your life, which may mean getting the professional help required.

FIVE GUIDEPOSTS

There are five guideposts to help you navigate your darkness:

1. Stand Together
2. Sit in the Dark
3. Find Hope to Turn on the Light
4. Step Out and Step Up
5. Open Your Heart to Love

Stand Together

The first guidepost in navigating the darkness is Stand Together.

Stand Together is about learning not to travel in the darkness alone. We all have moments of darkness, hurt, pain, loneliness, deep sorrow, even anguish in our lives. You are not alone, and neither do you have to go through your journey on your own. As you go through this book, know you will stand with many who have had experiences like yours. Their stories are provided as encouragement and guideposts to navigate your way towards your success.

When it's dark, you turn on the light. The lessons you learn here will become your light to help you navigate the darkness and understand how to turn on your light. The great thing is that once you discover your inner light, you will never be lost in darkness.

Loneliness is not simply just a sad condition—it can be a dangerous one. We, as human beings, need social connections. Navigating the darkness is more manageable when you stand with support. This idea is best expressed by this ancient saying: "A person standing alone can be attacked and defeated, but two can stand back-to-back and conquer. Three are even better, for a triple-braided cord is not easily broken."

EXERCISE

1. Who could I ask to journey with me and create my three-stranded cord?

   _____

   _____

   _____

   _____

2. Schedule time with those you listed, sit down, let them know of your goals, and ask for their support.

   _____

   _____

   _____

   _____

Sit in the Dark

Guidepost number two is Sit in the Dark.

I first understood absolute physical darkness as a teenager while on a caving trip. We descended into a vast cavern. When we reached the bottom of the cavern, it was dark, but a sliver of light came through the gap in the rocks. After a time, my eyes adjusted, and I could see each group member in the dim light.

We squeezed through narrow, muddy rock passages as we moved deeper into the cave. Finally, after half an hour of climbing, crawling, and walking, we came to a large cavern where there was enough space for us all to pause as a team. Our guides asked us to move close to one another. As we did, he explained why.

"In a moment, I'm going to ask you to turn off your flashlights. Then I want you to just sit in the dark."

The guide explained that it is perfectly normal for you to lose your balance in total darkness and that you may feel scared and disorientated. He told us that he wanted us to reach out and touch another person if we felt overwhelmed. He explained if someone reaches out to us, we are not to push them away or turn on our flashlight. The goal is to sit and get comfortable with the total darkness.

After what seemed like forever sitting in the darkness, our guide started talking. He asked whether we could see anything now that our eyes had time to adjust. The answer was no. He explained there was no natural light where we were in the cave, and therefore, our eyes would never adjust.

Our guide asked a few more questions to help us connect with this experience and the total darkness. Questions about how we felt in general and knowing we were just a few feet away from other people we could not see. He asked how knowing we could reach out and touch the person next to us felt. We then ate our lunch in this total darkness before moving on. It was a profound experience.

As much as you want to get out of the darkness, you may need to pause and sit for a while, look after your physical needs, then continue your journey when rested, as we did in that cave. Along your journey of success, you need to be prepared to sit in the dark, rest, and reflect on how you will move to the next level in your life.

I didn't realize it at the time, but that day, I learned lessons about darkness and light, connecting to others and myself, and fear and trust.

EXERCISE

Where are you in your journey as it relates to darkness?

- ☐ Never experienced darkness
- ☐ In darkness – feeling alone
- ☐ Reaching out to connect
- ☐ Pushing through on my own
- ☐ Navigating forward with help
- ☐ I can see the light ahead
- ☐ I'm out the other side of darkness and creating the life I dream of

Many cultures, families, and professional norms have drilled into our thinking that admitting pain or seeking help is a weakness. I have many friends in the military from whom I have heard the expression, "We don't get PTSD; we give it." This expression was to condition the person that they are tougher than the enemy. Deep down, each of these military persons has absorbed the thinking that vulnerability and acknowledgment of pain is weakness. Let me assure you that asking for help is one of the most courageous actions you can take.

EXERCISE

What is your most common response when faced with a highly stressful situation?

- ☐ Deny – Hide my feelings, keep pushing forward
- ☐ Fight – React with anger
- ☐ Blame – Blame others or the world
- ☐ Hide – Disconnect emotionally
- ☐ Shut down – Complete emotional and physical withdrawal
- ☐ Drown – Turn to drugs, alcohol, or other addictions such as busyness, shopping, eating, etc.
- ☐ Face Up – Take responsibility, get the help I need

Find Hope to Turn on the Light

The third guidepost is Find Hope to Turn on the Light.

As a ten-year-old, I experienced abuse from a family friend. As a result of this abuse, I was left feeling scared, lost, dirty, and believing what had happened to me was my fault. My perpetrator told me I must not say anything to anyone. So, I did nothing for six months and spoke to no one about what had happened. Then, one day, I finally broke and told my parents. My parents called the police, and there was an investigation. It was a hard time. In the end, the case was closed without going to court. The injustice was the laws favored the abuser, and putting a child on the stand was considered too stressful. So, no charges were filed without adult witnesses.

It was a dark time in my life. At first, when I was in my darkest place, I thought I would never trust again, never smile, never laugh, never feel safe again. But, speaking out and not hiding brought a measure of peace. I created a crack that allowed the first tiny light in by bringing my hurt into the open. As I grew older, I reached out to others to fuel hope, to grow and overcome the fear and hurt I felt. I wanted to live an abundant life. I hoped there was a way. Hope was not only a guidepost but a healer in this situation.

When I started reading, something began to shift in me. To my surprise, I found many, even most, of the people in the success stories I read had experienced trauma in their life, but despite the trauma, they had not gone under. The opposite happened. They used their trauma to push forward and thrive. Despite every horrible thing that happened to them, these people had succeeded instead of being defeated.

These stories gave me hope, knowing that if they could do it, so could I. But more than that, for me, it was a revelation. My experience didn't have to define me. It didn't have to limit me. What I hoped for in my life was possible. Having to live in darkness was not my future. So, the light within me started to burn brighter. Much like how news of Roger Bannister breaking the four-minute mile gave other runners the hope and courage to break through what appeared impossible, the stories of other people's trauma gave me the hope and courage to break free of my darkness and create my better life.

What is something you lost hope in that now seems possible?

_____

_____

_____

_____

_____

Step Out and Step Up

The fourth guidepost is Step Out and Step Up.

As I researched stories of people who had been through hell and back to understand why some thrived and others didn't, I wanted to know, *What makes the difference? What can I learn from those who thrived to help me thrive?* What I discovered are a few common threads. These common threads helped me develop my "Five Guideposts Through the Darkness" and "The Four Paths Model" that you are learning in part in this book. The impact of darkness, the feeling of shame, and the cry for worthiness and connection were intrinsic to the stories. The journey out of the darkness was a mental, emotional, and physical growth journey. Each person had to step out in hope and up in courage. With hope, I stepped up my learning, and with courage, I stepped out of my comfort zone, using the guideposts I discovered in the stories.

One key difference I found in the success stories after trauma was that the people who thrived decided they would thrive! They decided their life would be different, then followed their decision with action to make it happen.

Their actions were as varied as the people and their specific situations. Some chose to move away from a hostile environment, even when that meant starting over with nothing. Others sought treatment. Others changed their actions and thinking. Many found role models and mentors to help them on their journey. All took personal responsibility for themselves—their thinking, past actions, and future actions. They owned their change.

EXERCISE

Where do you need to step out and step up?

_____

_____

_____

_____

Open Your Heart to Love

Guidepost number five is Open Your Heart to Love.

Marianne Williamson describes the impact of opening your heart to love so beautifully: "Light is to darkness what love is to fear; in the presence of one, the other disappears."

One afternoon, I was visiting my dad at the hospital. His face was tired and worn. This visit, like our relationship, was not easy. My relationship with my dad had been challenging for several years. He always described himself as "a self-made man" who had risen from tough beginnings. Work was his safe place and source of self-worth throughout his life. When faced with stress, particularly in relationships, he didn't cope well and turned to work as his refuge. A tour in Vietnam in 1970 as part of a civilian medical team had changed him in a way that I later would understand as Post-Traumatic Stress Disorder (PTSD).

Dad moved his coping mechanism from workaholism to alcoholism when I was a teen. That switch resulted in his poor health and this stay in the hospital. He was my dad, and I loved him, even though I didn't like how he acted sometimes and hated some of the things he said and did. So, I decided to sit with him at the hospital. As I sat beside him, I saw a shadow of the father I once knew. For the first time in a very long time, he opened up and talked about the hurt, sorrow, and grief he had experienced and inflicted. I listened. He shared that he saw how I had a heart full of love. That evening, he said he had often wished he could have faith and know love as I did, and he wished he could pray, but he didn't believe in God. After he finished sharing, I suggested if he wanted to pray, he simply needed to be real and be himself. I told him, "Ask God if He's there, if He's real, to help you know Him and to know love." My dad prayed from his heart to Wendy's God that night, possibly for the first time. He prayed to know love.

Some say you can see the soul of a person through their eyes. After my dad opened his heart in prayer that night, I saw the change in his eyes. There was a peace that had not been there before. Then, two days later, he passed away. The darkness had gone from his eyes, but the years of self-abuse took their toll in the end.

Don't wait till you are dying to open your heart to love. Love of and for your family. Love of humanity. Love of nature. If you desire it, God's love. There is so much more to life when you open your heart to love. With a heart open to love, you may still experience times of darkness, but you will be able to navigate through those times with a different strength.

LEARNING AND MOVING FORWARD - THE FOUR PATHS.

On Tuesday, January 18, 1977, a crowded commuter train derailed in Granville, Australia. Known as the Granville train disaster, the crash claimed 83 lives and injured 213 others. This derailment changed lives and legislation. The ripples spread far and wide. The media called it The Disaster That Changed Australia.

Forty years later, when I sought to understand why some people come out of a disaster and thrive while others do not, the understanding of that disaster became the foundation for a model for, The Four Paths.

What became apparent was that those who recovered and moved forward after the train crash didn't take just one path. Instead, they used all four paths available to them.

EMERGING FROM THE DARKNESS – THE FOUR PATHS.

There were four primary responses to the event, which I call The Four Paths.

Paths 1 and 2 are the "Fix It" paths.

Path 1. Organizational and Infrastructure: Someone external to me fixes things external to me.

In the case of The Disaster That Changed Australia, the government and relevant institutions held inquiries. They looked at what had gone wrong. They fixed the railway, and new regulations, systems, policies, and procedures were implemented to prevent reoccurrence. In addition, the government made finances available to fix the problem and provide support to the injured.

Path 2. Medical People: Those external to me fix me.

Hospitals, local doctors, psychologists, counselors, and first aid providers all played their part. Immediately after the event and continuing for a long time, the medical path helped lead people out of trauma and heal people who were hurt.

Paths one and two are external paths and system-based paths. In my research, I noticed some people waited for the organization, the government, or medical people to fix their situation and to fix them. There was the attitude, "They broke me. They need to fix me." But that attitude brought its problems. The stories showed when you rely on only "fix it" paths, you remain a victim. The best outcome you can expect with paths one and two is survival.

Paths 3 and 4 are the Personal Responsibility paths.

Path 3. Personal Decision: I choose me. I feed me.

Here is where the difference showed up between those who went on to thrive and those who struggled. Those who went on to thrive chose to take the initiative and responsibility for their life and future. They used all the resources available to them but were not limited by them. They sought out what and who they needed to help them. They said things like, "I'm not waiting for somebody or some department to do this. I'll do what it takes. I'll find what I need. I don't know how, but I will." Personal decision, personal responsibility. I choose!

Some people decided not to let that dark experience ruin their lives. Instead, they held hope for a better outcome in the third path, and they pursued it. Their pain became their reason. Their pain became their power.

Path 4. Companion Path: We walk together.

In my original model, there were only three paths. Then, my colleague, Dr. Dorothy Bonvillain, told me that I needed a fourth path—a path that included the family and loved ones. When I looked again at the stories of those that thrived, Dorothy was right. The fourth path was about those who loved and cared for the person coming out of the darkness. Companions can love and encourage someone, but they cannot do what the person must do themselves.

EXERCISE

1. Think of your darkest experiences. Which paths will you choose to move forward today?

_____

_____

_____

_____

2. What is the next right action you need to take?

_____

_____

_____

HELPING THE INVISIBLE BE SEEN

It's far too easy not to understand or believe what you cannot see. But I have observed that wisdom gained from what we can see can help us understand and better respond to what we cannot see. So, I use the train crash concept as a starting point because it is easy to picture, comprehend, and apply understanding.

Think of an experience when you sensed, maybe even knew, something was wrong, but you were not sure exactly what. Did you know how to respond?

I broke my arm in primary school and had a plaster cast from my wrist to my underarm. People could see my plaster cast and adjust their expectations of me accordingly.

What is the difference between someone with a broken or amputated limb, someone wearing a cast prosthesis or in a wheelchair, and someone with depression, PTSD, anxiety, or any other injury of the mind? What is the difference between the visible and the invisible injury? The difference is that a physical injury provides a visual trigger for someone else to see, create understanding, and guide appropriate expectations.

When you experience an invisible injury, it is your opportunity to share what's happening inside of you and create understanding. It creates an opportunity to help others become aware and understand what they can't see. I know sharing may not be easy, particularly if you do not fully understand what's happening yourself. It is no one's fault they cannot see, understand, or respond how you want them to. They simply don't have the information they need. To share the unseen requires courage and vulnerability on your part.

EXERCISE

What different ways can you share what you are feeling/experiencing to create greater understanding?

_____

_____

_____

_____

_____

SUMMARY

- Everyone experiences darkness.
- The trigger of your darkness will be personal.
- The feelings of experiencing darkness are human.
- When you light your light within, you will never experience total darkness again.
- The Five Principles for navigating the darkness are:
    1. Stand Together
    2. Sit in the Dark
    3. Find Hope to Turn on the Light
    4. Step Out and Step Up
    5. Open Your Heart to Love
- The Four Paths leading out of the darkness in your life:
    1. Organizational and Infrastructure
    2. Medical
    3. Personal Decision
    4. Companion
- Each path has a role to play.
- To thrive, access all paths.

Chapter 4
Journeying in the Light

"When you arise in the morning, think of what a precious privilege it is to be alive – to breathe, to think, to enjoy, to love."
Marcus Aurelius

We talked about navigating through and overcoming the darkness. Now, let's discover the adventure of journeying in the light.

Journeying means to travel somewhere. Your journey to your success will challenge you to become a better version of yourself and, in doing so, take you to new places. We have noted that some parts of our journey are laborious and slow because we sometimes travel in the darkness. However, when we travel in the light, we can see clearly and go faster, more safely, and efficiently because we can see where we are going.

Sight is biology. Vision is a choice. When you have sight, you can see where you are going. When you have vision, you can see beyond your physical limits and walk in the light of the vision, even when it is far away. Your vision—that picture in your mind of what your success looks like—will light your path so you can see the way to go. When you see your path, you can choose well where to take the next step.

Walking in the light gives you confidence. Have you ever tried hiking at night? The darkness can be scary without the moon, stars, or city lights. It can be easy to come down wrong on a foot and end up with a broken ankle. It is easy to become lost, easy to imagine the worst. In the darkness, it is easy to give up.

In the light, you can see where you are and the challenges you face. You can find your bearings, choose a new direction, and plan your onward journey.

You can see who is with you and connect with them to journey together.

EXERCISE

What is your picture of success?

_____

_____

_____

_____

If you struggle with the idea of success, start by asking yourself what is most important for you. Knowing what you value is an excellent starting point for creating your definition of your success.

COMING, READY OR NOT

Adventure requires doing new things. It requires moving outside your comfort zone and into the unknown. An adventurous journey has excitement mingled with a bit of fear. Even when you have prepared for the journey, it can be easy not to feel ready, especially when you don't know what to expect.

EXERCISE

Think of the most exciting moments in your life. Did you feel ready? What were your expectations?

1. List the top five exciting moments you have experienced.

_____

_____

_____

_____

_____

2. On a scale of 1 to 10, how prepared did you feel for those moments?

_____

When I sat down and did this exercise for the first time, I noticed that my most exciting moments were many of the most unexpected. It felt like life was playing a childhood game, calling out, "Coming, ready or not."

One f the most exciting moments in my life was my first solo flight. I was at the Bankstown Airport in Sydney at 6 a.m. on what would be a scorching day. I had been told the heat would rise by midday, which would create lots of turbulence—not ideal conditions for novice pilots. I still needed the relative stillness of the early morning to fly safely.

As usual, my instructor was seated next to me. I taxied out to the runway and took off, flew a circuit of the airport, and did what's called a touch-and-go. A touch-and-go is when you land, then push on the throttle and take off again without actually coming to a stop. It's a valuable skill to have during emergencies. I did a few more touch-and-go. As I prepared to land, I heard my instructor talking to the control tower in a muffled voice. I landed and started taxiing off the runway.

Mid-taxiway, my instructor said, "Stop here."

I looked at him, confused. I was thinking, *Here? We are in the middle of the airport's taxiway.*

Then he said, "I'm getting out. I'll walk back to the hanger. I want you to take off on your own, complete a circuit, land, and taxi back to the hanger."

Hearing him say this made the butterflies in my stomach take flight but not in formation. Fear and excitement were mixed. The fight-or-flight response, fueled by the adrenaline in my system, took on new meaning at that moment. I swallowed. I took a deep breath. I didn't feel ready, but my instructor believed in me. I had prepared for this moment. I knew the day would come. Now it was here. I was scared, and I was excited. So, with both excitement and fear, I started my first solo. I did what I had learned to do.

I completed the pre-takeoff checks, lined up the plane on the runway, and with the tower's call, "Clear for takeoff," I opened the throttle and headed down the runway. I pulled back on the controls, and I was flying. At the approved height, I turned left and joined the circuit. On "final," I prepared to land while calling off in my head the landing checklist:

- Flaps – check.
- Confirm approach with the tower – check.
- Flight attitude nose down – check.
- Reduce speed – check.
- Power level for control – check.
- Center the plane over the white stripes that mark the end of the runway – check.
- Landing attitude – check.
- Touchdown – check.
- Brake evenly – check.
- Slow and pull onto the taxiway – check.

I did it! I flew solo!

Safely touching down was such an emotional moment. The sense of relief and achievement was just incredible. Then, over the radio came, "Romeo Sierra Papa," the callsign of my plane.

For a split second, like a child, I thought, *Oh no, what is the matter? What did I forget? What did I do wrong?*

Then from the control tower, I heard, "Congratulations."

When my instructor got out of the aircraft and left me alone, the physical symptoms of fear and excitement rose. I had to choose. Would I push past fear and lean into excitement? I decided to face my fear, focus on the excitement, and do what I needed to do.

The energy and emotions of fear make sense when you need to run from a lion in the wilderness or other life-threatening situations. But, in everyday life, false fear can steal your focus and block your success.

Recently, I came across a study that said it takes eight seconds of courage to overcome a moment of fear. Those eight seconds allow for the adrenaline spike associated with fear to fade. Holding the idea of courage for eight seconds allows the thinking part of your brain to reconnect. Those eight seconds help you retake control and choose the right thing, do the right thing, and move forward. Only eight seconds of courage required!

Those eight seconds of courage describe my first solo flight experience perfectly. When the feelings of fear and doubt—driven by the adrenaline—took over my body, it felt like forever for me to settle into what I needed to do. However, I just needed eight seconds. Eight seconds echo my grandmother's advice, who always reminded me to "count to ten" when angry or scared before doing anything. Counting to ten gives your brain the eight seconds it needs to re-engage your thinking brain, act with clarity, and go for the success before you.

STRENGTHENING COURAGE

With my first solo flight, three things helped strengthen my courage.

1. Preparation – I knew I had prepared well.
2. Borrowed belief – I knew my instructor believed in me, and he was the expert!
3. Belief in myself – I believed I could do it because of the first two points.

By building my courage, fear became excitement, and the solo flight was a challenge I could rise to.

FACING YOUR FEAR OPENS NEW DOORS

I experienced an ending and a new beginning with my first solo over. Now there was more to learn. I was ready to move past the mechanics of flying and learn about navigation. My flying could take me beyond flying laps around the airfield. Because I had faced my fears with eight seconds of courage, a new world was about to open. I guess you could say the sky was indeed the limit now.

A phrase I use often is "Action cures fear." When I face the unknown, I ask myself, *What action do I need to take? What is the next right thing to do in this situation?* Other phrases learned over the years come to mind encouraging me to move past fear. Phrases like, "Do it afraid," and "Jump and build your wings on the down." Writing this book is a cliff jump for me. I feel vulnerable and scared, but I'm doing it anyway because if this book helps one person face their fears and create a better future, it is worth it.

EXERCISE

1. What has stopped you in the past?

   _____

   _____

   _____

   _____

2. Where can eight seconds of courage help you move forward?

   _____

   _____

   _____

   _____

GIVE YOURSELF PERMISSION

Remember in school when you had to take home a permission slip? No signed permission slip, no field trip. Are you ready to start your adventure? Or are you waiting for permission?

My favorite permission slip story comes from Dr. Brene Brown in her book, *Braving the Wilderness*. Dr. Brown was going to meet Oprah. She was so excited and a bit stressed out about it. When her manager called her out on being stressed, Brene admitted she was doing what she often did when she was afraid—floating above life, watching it, rather than living it. On hearing that, her manager told her, "This is a big deal. I don't want you to miss it. Don't study this moment. Be in it."

Brene says it was the following morning, while she was preparing to meet Oprah, that a text arrived from her daughter asking if she had returned the permission slip for her school trip. Brene says, "In that moment, I started thinking, I need to give myself a permission slip to stop being so serious and afraid. I need to give myself permission to have fun today." So, that is what she did. She wrote herself a permission slip on a Post-it Note that said, "Permission to be excited and goofy and to have fun today."

When I read that story, I cried and laughed. After that, I needed to write myself one of those permission slips! Brene says the permission slip would be the first of hundreds of permission slips she would write for herself. I also use the permission slips trick as an intention-setting practice in my own life.

My suggestion is don't wait for someone to give you permission to start and enjoy your adventure. Sit down right now and write yourself a permission slip to do whatever you need to!

EXERCISE

Take a moment and write out a permission slip for today for moving forward.

_____

_____

_____

_____

GROWING IN THE LIGHT

I would also like to tell you don't wait to be perfect or perfectly ready before you start. You will increase your clarity and build your strength as you go. Embrace your idea of success and take your next step, and you will see further along your path. You can learn whatever you need to know along the way. You can be more and achieve more when you are in motion. As you start, you will become more and more the person who can live your dream and navigate your path to success.

One of my favorite authors is cartoonist Theodore Geisel, known as Dr. Seuss. As Dr. Seuss wrote in *Oh, The Places You'll Go!* — "Be your name Buxbaum or Bixby or Bray…you're off to great places! Today is your day! Your mountain is waiting, so get on your way!"

Are you ready? Go and discover the places you can go!

SUMMARY

- Your journey is an adventure, complete with difficulty and danger.
- Sight is biology. Vision is choice.
- Light shows you where you are.
- Journeying in the light is faster, easier, and safer.
- Vision is your picture of success that allows you to see where to go, even if it is far away.
- Practice eight seconds of courage.
- Permit yourself to be you, be present, have fun, and be a little goofy.
- You can learn what you need.
- Today is your day. Get on your way!

SET

Chapter 5
Knowing and Loving You

"People travel to wonder at the height of mountains, at the huge waves of the sea, at the long courses of rivers, at the vast compass of the ocean, at the circular motion of the stars; and they pass by themselves without wondering."
Saint Augustine

In the first chapters of this book, we talked about getting READY. Now, in these next few chapters, it is all about you and getting yourself SET to maximize your adventure and your success. This chapter, *Knowing and Loving You*, is to open you to the wonder that is you and from wonder to knowledge and love. Knowing and loving you is the foundation of learning and living what's important. Knowing and loving you connects you to your success. Yet, knowing and loving yourself is not common nor easy. It is something most of the world struggles to do.

Knowing and loving you affects not only you but every connection you make with your world. When you know and love yourself, you can truly understand what it means to be you and to belong. Research shows the link between knowing and loving yourself and belonging. *True belonging* is defined as "the innate human desire to be part of something larger than us" that "only happens when we present our authentic, imperfect selves to the world." You can only do that when you know and love yourself. Your sense of belonging and community will never be greater than your level of self-acceptance. Seeking approval and trying to fit in are both hollow substitutes for truly belonging that often limit us. You can't be perfect. You don't have to be perfect. You can be authentic. You can be you. Don't try and be someone else in the vain hope of fitting in.

I was once asked by my mentor, "Why are you trying to fit in when you were made to stand out?" You are enough! In knowing and loving who you are, you permit yourself—and open the door—to grow and become even better.

Your value is not diminished by your imperfections, by what you have experienced, or by the way you feel. Taking the time to know and love yourself is not easy or something to be glossed over. And it is not a one-time event. It is a process. As you grow and learn, you can appreciate the wonder that is you more fully and love yourself more.

For now, I want to introduce you to three aspects of knowing and loving you and how to discover and live what's most important to you.

Knowing your

1. Worth; your intrinsic value
2. Unique design; the way you were made
3. Your choices; your important

KNOWING YOUR WORTH

Picture this. I am holding up a one-hundred-dollar bill and say, "Here's one hundred dollars." Then I scrunch the bill into a tight ball, put the money under my foot, and stomp on it. Next, I go outside and rub the hundred dollars in the dirt.

I then ask, "Would you still want it? If so, why?"

When I use the bill demonstration in a workshop, without fail, someone answers, "To have one hundred dollars." Why? Because its value is intrinsic, meaning the value cannot be separated from what it is. This is true for you, too! You are far more valuable than money. Your value is not diminished by your experiences, your feelings, or the opinions of others. You are worth far more than you possibly can even think or imagine. Even better, you can add value to yourself daily by developing yourself, your knowledge, and your skills.

Social media today fuels impossible expectations. It makes it look like everybody else out there is a new, crisp one-hundred-dollar bill—not scrunched or stomped on. And that somehow that crisp one-hundred-dollar bill is better, more valuable than my other one-hundred-dollar bill. Not true. Like that one hundred dollars, your value cannot be separated from who you are. Your value was determined when you were created and remains, regardless of what has happened since. To believe anything else is to accept a bogus story, a lie. You are unique and immensely valuable. You were made that way.

EXERCISE

I would like you to take two actions today and then repeat daily till the messages are part of who you are.

1. Today, look at a family member with eyes of love. As you look at them, say in your mind, "You are valuable. You are worth it. You are worthy of love and belonging. I love you."

2. Today, look at yourself in the mirror with eyes of love. As you look at your reflection, say to yourself, "You are valuable. You are worth it. You are worthy of love and belonging. I love you."

I placed them in this order because often, it is easier to find the value in others before finding the value in ourselves.

UNDERSTANDING YOUR UNIQUE DESIGN

You are unique. And understanding your unique design can be a liberating and empowering experience.

For a long time, I felt trapped, as though I was a genie in a bottle—trapped and a slave to the whims and desires of others. I wanted out. I knew there was more to life than the tiny confines others had for me.

But what could I do? Where would I start? What would others think of me if suddenly I started living and believing differently? I found the answers started with understanding my unique design—the way I'm wired.

William Moulton Marston was an American psychologist, inventor, and writer. Marston recognized that while we are individuals, we are unique and show predictable behavior patterns. From his research, he created the *D.I.S.C. Model of Normal Human Behaviour.*

The D.I.S.C. model is like finding a map to understand yourself and others and creating positive relationships. The map first creates awareness, then understanding, then appreciation of yourself and others so you can celebrate your uniqueness. The insights I gained from completing a D.I.S.C. Personality Assessment totally surprised me and exhilarated me. The new awareness and understanding I received helped me relate better to my husband, children, and colleagues. It helped me…

1. Understand the box I was in .
2. Escape that box.
3. Grow myself.
4. Understand others better and build stronger relationships.
5. Make better choices based on who I really was.
6. Stop taking offense when no offense was meant.
7. Experience more joy in life.

If you would like to understand more of your unique design and experience more joy, you can find a link in the back of the book to take your D.I.S.C. Personality Assessment.

FROM YOUR STRENGTHS

As well as unique wiring, you have your unique strengths. We all do. To live more fully in our potential, we need to grow our strengths. But, before you can grow them, you have to know them. Sounds simple, but how do you start?

The first step is to be open. That may require you to get out of your own way. Strengths are not good or bad, right or wrong. They just are. Self-esteem issues can block you from seeing or acknowledging your strengths. Others can often help you find your strengths, especially when you can't see them yourself.

EXERCISE

1. Write a list of what you currently think of as your strengths.
2. Ask others to make a list of your strengths.
3. Compare the lists. Look for the commonality and note the differences.

4. Reflect on what you have discovered.

If there is something on the other's list, don't dismiss it. Take a moment and ask them to give you an example and then thank them. Often, we fail to see the strengths others see in us. Having them give you an example will help you see your strength in action.

Understand that finding your strength is part of the bigger process of knowing and loving yourself. It is a process of discovery and growth, not judgment. Do not judge yourself. Don't judge the responses others gave you. The process will involve trial and error, but partnering with the right people can make it easier, faster, and more fun. By finding and building on your strengths, it will be easier to produce the consistent growth and results that create your success.

BUILDING IN ALIGNMENT

When you build a home, the walls and ceiling need to be built in alignment. Things need to match up for the structure to withstand the elements. Same with you. If your strengths and values are not in alignment, it weakens your ability to remain stable and strong in times of challenge.

From time to time, stop and ask yourself, "Is there alignment between my personality, strengths, talents, dreams, and values? If not, you will be wasting your time, energy, and effort. Because when the times get tough and the darkness moves in, you will not be able to withstand it.

Think about it. If you have excellent musical abilities, a dream to be a concert pianist is realistic but still requires hard work. People and companies pay well for excellence, not for mediocrity. You can develop excellence when your starting talent is eight or nine out of ten.

Trying to grow your weakness instead of your strengths puts you in the position of forever working but never winning. Your unique talents and strengths are part of what makes you uniquely you. I understand it takes time and effort to discover and develop them, but I encourage you to keep going until you do. Your talents and strengths are key to your success.

EXERCISE

1. Write a list of the strengths you will focus on developing. (Minimum 3, maximum 5)

_____

_____

_____

_____

2. How will developing these strengths help you achieve your dreams?

_____

_____

_____

_____

CHOOSING YOUR IMPORTANT

Once you understand how you are uniquely designed (your strengths and talents), you are ready to better understand what is most important for you; what you value and what you choose. Choosing what you value contributes to getting to know and love yourself and your success.

Have you heard of Scott Harrison or his charity, *Charity Water?* I heard Scott interviewed by Brene Brown as part of her *Daring Interview Series.* What stood out to me was how his choices and experiences molded the person Scott Harrison has become.

Today, everything about Scott looks great. He is recognized on *Fortune Magazine's* "40 under 40" list and *Forbes* "Impact 30" list. It is hard to think of Scott Harrison as someone who did not like himself. However, Scott says, "I was the worst person I knew."

A little more than ten years prior to this interview, Scott worked as a nightclub promoter in New York. He describes his life then as "revolving around smoking, drugs, models, and heavy drinking." Scott says while most people thought he had it all, he came to realize he had nothing of real value. The turning point in his life came when Scott realized, "I had become the worst version of myself. I was morally bankrupt, not living the values I grew up believing."

In response to his new awareness, Scott Harrison asked himself three questions:

1. A Vision Question – "What would the exact opposite of my life look like?"
2. A Values Question – "What might it look like to return to the morality and spirituality of my youth?"
3. A Legacy Question – "What might it look like to serve others instead of myself?"

As a result, Scott volunteered as a photojournalist on a humanitarian medical mission in West Africa six months later. While on that trip, Scott saw the connection between contaminated water and disease. He discovered dirty water was the source of more death and disease than war. What astounded him was that water was something he took for granted back home. Scott became fired up to do something about access to water and started *Charity Water*, which now brings clean water to communities in twenty-six different countries.

What does Scott's story teach us? Choices have consequences! Scott's early choices made him money, but not a life he was proud to live. Once he had awareness, he shifted his priorities. Scott started building a life he could be proud of—a life where he could find joy and fulfillment.

Are you proud of yourself and your life? Are you living your core values?

To make good choices about what is important in your life, start by asking yourself the three big questions Scott asked himself. You don't have to wait or take a trip to discover what is most important for you and start your transformation journey. However, when you consider potentially life-changing questions like these, changing your environment can be very helpful, even if only a few hours. Your current environment can trigger habitual thinking. A new environment can provide space for reflection and new ideas to challenge what needs to change. Even if you have asked yourself these essential questions before, take the opportunity now to reflect again, then course-correct as required.

EXERCISE

1. Vision: The best version of my life looks like…

_____
_____
_____
_____

2. Values: Living my core values looks like…

_____
_____
_____
_____

3. Purpose: Serving others instead of myself looks like…

_____
_____
_____
_____

4. Planning: Five things I need to change to live my best life are…

_____
_____
_____
_____

5. Two actions I will take now to start the process are…

_____

_____

_____

_____

DECIDING WHAT REALLY MATTERS

Facing death can push you to view life differently and see what is most important for you. Two men, two very similar stories, two opposite outcomes. One on a twisting Caribbean Road, and the other on a broad Australian Highway.

Imagine you are driving along, listening to great music. All is okay in your world; then your car goes into a spin. The next moment, your life passes before your eyes in slow motion. What would the movie of your life look like? These two men experienced this scenario.

Tom was driving in Australia. He had a family and a business, and his life was pretty good. Then crash! His life flashed before his eyes. The car was totaled, and Tom's recovery was a long, slow process.

After breaking up with his girlfriend, Brendon was hurting badly emotionally. To give himself space, he traveled with a friend to the Caribbean to work on a service project. They were driving back to their accommodation when the car rolled over.

Two men, two car crashes. Two lives almost lost—both given a second chance. There the similarities end. Tom decided life could be taken away at any time and therefore felt life had no meaning other than to "eat, drink and be merry." As a result of his near-death experience, Tom decided the only important thing for Tom was Tom himself. Life became Tom first, Tom second, Tom everything. He became self-centered and controlling. He spent money on fast cars and high living. Eventually, he lost his family and health. When his family tried to reconnect, they found a dying, unhappy man who burned with anger at everyone and everything.

Brendon, on the other hand, reflected on his life and came up with a different response. He asked himself three life-changing questions: "Did I live? Did I love? Did I matter?" Facing the near-death moment, Brendon realized he had another chance at life and a choice to build a life that mattered or keep going as before. Even during his rehabilitation, Brendon experienced new clarity and joy. He saw life was filled with hope and opportunity. For Brendon, his experience led him to create a life of contribution to others, to grow to his maximum potential, and to build strong, loving relationships. Brendon writes of his car crash and its impact on his life in his book, *Life's Golden Ticket*.

It's time to start living your important starting now. Whatever is happening in your life, stop and ask yourself if your task is important for you.

Stop waiting till everything is perfect to chase your hopes, dreams, and success. Let me tell you a secret. Things will never be perfect. The good news is they don't have to be—and neither do you.

EXERCISE

1. If today was the last day of your life, what would be most important for you to do?

   _____

   _____

   _____

   _____

2. What do you want people to say about you and your life when you are not here?

   _____

   _____

   _____

   _____

START IN THE MIRROR

You don't have to have a car accident or face a near-death situation to make the decision to be the best you or to decide what's most important for you. You can choose right now. Invest the time. Become curious. Figure it out. It may be the greatest time investment you ever make.

ACTIVITY

Start to change yourself by looking in the mirror. This action won't be easy, but do it anyway!

1. Go and face the person in the mirror.
2. Answer the questions below.
    a. How would you describe the person you see?
    b. What is that person's greatest talent or gift?
    c. What are the qualities of the person looking back at you?
    d. Do you trust them? Why? Why not? When? When not?
    e. What do you think was most important for them in the past?
    f. What could you learn from the person in the mirror to make your life better?
3. Tell the person in the mirror you love them and will care for them each and every day moving forward.

EXERCISE

1. While looking in the mirror, I would tell the person I see, "Your best qualities are…"

   _____
   _____
   _____
   _____

2. I would tell the person in the mirror, "The lessons I learned

from you last year to move forward this year are…"

_____

_____

_____

_____

BELONGING TO SELF

The person who decides what is important in your life controls your life. Have you seen the movie *Chariots of Fire*? It is the story of two runners, Eric Liddell and Harold Abrahams, part of the British team in the 1924 Paris Olympics. When I think of people who struggled to fit in yet found true belonging, I think of Eric Liddell.

Eric Liddell was called the "Flying Scotsman" because he ran so fast! Born in China to missionary parents, he was enrolled in a boarding school in south London at the age of six. Liddell earned "Athlete of the Year." His headmaster described him as being a "great athlete who was entirely without vanity."

While at the University of Edinburgh, he ran in the 100-yard and the 220-yard. Liddell soon became famous for being the fastest runner in Scotland. Newspapers carried stories of his feats at track meets, and many articles stated he was a potential Olympic winner. In the movie, *Chariots of Fire*, his character is quoted as saying, "I believe God made me for a purpose, but He also made me fast. And when I run, I feel His pleasure."

He qualified for the 100-meter in the Olympics as a member of the British Athletics team. When Eric learned the 100-meter heats would be run on a Sunday, he faced a conflict, as running on a Sunday went against who he was and what he stood for. The movie highlights Eric Liddell's dilemma and the intense pressure brought to bear on Eric to change his mind. Belonging to a team came with expectations, as did belonging to himself. Belonging to yourself requires the strength to stand alone. Eric Liddell was prepared to stand alone. Eric Liddell chose not to run in the 100-meter, but with support from a fellow team member, he switched to the 400-meter competition, winning the gold medal.

More tough decisions followed. Returning to Edinburgh, Eric graduated, trained, and was accepted as a missionary to China. When World War II came to China, Eric didn't return to his native Scotland, and in 1943, Eric was interred at a Prisoner of War camp where he died. When news of his death reached Scotland, it was reported that all of Scotland mourned.

Through those struggles and tests, Eric learned who he was and what he stood for. He understood what was most important for him. He was prepared to stand alone for who he was and what he believed. He had boundaries he would not cross. To cross them would be to lose his identity, self-respect, and the power that allowed him to dig so deep and run so fast.

You will confront your own tough decisions and be required to make difficult decisions on your journey. Others will seek to influence and control you. Their expectations may be against what you desire, believe in, and stand for. Eric left a legacy because he knew himself. He understood true belonging is not about fitting in; it is about belonging to yourself first. Will you dig deep and find your true belonging? Will you make decisions on what is truly important for you?

EXERCISE

1. What are two things you stand for that you will not compromise?

   _____

   _____

   _____

   _____

2. What boundaries do you need to establish regarding things you stand for and believe in?

   _____

   _____

   _____

SUMMARY

- Knowing and loving you is the secret to your success.
- It takes courage and love to accept your imperfect self and move ahead anyway.
- Your sense of belonging can never be greater than your level of self-acceptance.
- Knowing yourself includes knowing your:
    1. Worth, your intrinsic value
    2. Unique design, the way you were made
    3. Your important
- You start trapped in a box; you stay there until you understand yourself and climb out.
- Your choices create your life and future.
- Align your strengths and talents with your dreams and work.
- Changing your environment, even temporarily, can open up space to evaluate your life and make positive changes.
- If you do not pick what you stand for and believe in, someone else will pick it for you.
- The person who chooses your important controls your life.
- When you belong to yourself, you set appropriate boundaries.
- When you belong to yourself, you have the courage to stand alone.

Chapter 6
Building Your Strength

"With the new day comes new strength and new thoughts."
Eleanor Roosevelt

Congratulations! The last chapter required a lot of heavy lifting as you looked at knowing, loving, and valuing yourself. No matter how much we wish it didn't, life always has challenges. You may start your journey towards success with passion but fail to finish if you lack the strength to do what is needed. In this chapter, you will look at how you build your strength, physical and inner, to start your journey well, withstand pressure, and navigate through challenges to complete your journey well.

The good news is you can always level up your mental, emotional, and physical strength. Building your strength and success go hand in hand because you are the only person you can control. This chapter will focus on what you can do daily to strengthen yourself and make you better tomorrow than you are today. Strength is not static. Stop building your strength, and you will lose your strength. Thus why building your strength daily is so important.

To strengthen you, first, strengthen your thinking. You will always end up where your thinking takes you. Your life today results from where your past thinking and decisions have brought you. So, new thinking is required to take you in a new direction.

BUILDING STRENGTH STARTS IN YOU

Susie Maroney was an Australian distance swimmer. When Susie was three years old, her parents enrolled her in a swimming program to help strengthen her breathing to help control her asthma attacks. At fifteen years of age, she had become the youngest Aussie to swim the English Channel. Susie achieved six world records, was twice inducted into the International Swimming Hall of Fame, and made the Guinness Book of Records for the longest distance swim over a twenty-four-hour period.

But Susie didn't start with the thinking, skills, and strength required to be a long-distance swimmer. She began like everyone else does when they first learn to swim. As she swam, her skills and strength increased. When she was thirteen, she realized she could swim long distances. It was then she shifted her goal from just being able to swim and developed the mental and physical strength needed to become a competitive long-distance swimmer. Susie put in hours of training, swimming lap after lap, building the endurance needed for the seventeen hours required to swim across the English Channel. The Susie Maroney who crossed the English Channel was not the same person, mentally and physically, as the three-year-old who took up swimming to control her asthma.

Your success, like Susie's, requires you to become a stronger version of who you are now. On the journey, you will be strengthened and transformed. Author James Clear, in Atomic Habits, says, "The power behind behavior change is changing the way you see yourself, your identity. True behavior change is identity change." You have done the foundational work of knowing and loving yourself first. Identity, beliefs, thoughts, actions, and results are all tied together. Strengthen your identity, and it will flow through and strengthen your results.

WORKING WITH YOURSELF

When you understand that how you think of yourself determines your behaviors and results, you can start working *with* yourself for your success and stop working *against* yourself. How you self-identify builds your habits, and your habits feed your identity, creating a feedback loop. Susie's long swims fed her declared identity as a long-distance swimmer. As she began to see herself as a long-distance swimmer, Susie's focus, workouts, and behavior in other areas of her life shifted.

James Clear illustrates the "change your identity, and you will change your behavior" principle. Two people are trying to give up smoking. When asked if they would like a cigarette, each responds differently. Within the response is the key to their non-smoking success.

- First response: "No, thanks. I'm trying to quit."
- Second response: "No, thanks. I'm not a smoker."

One ex-smoker still identified as a smoker. The second identified as a non-smoker. Of the two, which one do you think is more likely to succeed?

Words have power. The words you use are a window to how you see yourself. The way you think about yourself is reflected in your words to describe yourself and speak to yourself. If you stop and examine your words and change the words you use, you start the process of building your strength.

EXERCISE

1. What words do you use when talking about yourself to others?

   _____

   _____

   _____

   _____

2. What words do you tell yourself when no one else is listening?

   _____

   _____

   _____

   _____

WHO DO YOU THINK YOU ARE?

Think about your life. Can you see the relationship between your beliefs, actions, and results? I understand it is not always easy to see. It can be subtle, but it is there. Building strength is a process.

BELIEF | THINKING | ACTION | HABIT | RESULT

- To change your results, change your habits.
- To change your habits, change your actions.

- To change your actions, change your thinking.
- To change your thinking, change your beliefs.
- To change your beliefs, change the words you speak to yourself.

Suzie's story started with the belief that swimming would help her with asthma. Her beliefs about herself as a swimmer changed throughout her journey until finally becoming a set of beliefs that sounded like, "I am a long-distance swimmer." This change in her beliefs changed her thinking. With her changed thinking, her actions changed. Susie would spend more time doing the actions required of a successful long-distance swimmer. Those new actions became the habits that gave her the strength to achieve the result of swimming the English Channel.

Determination and willpower only go so far in creating change. Studies have shown it is difficult to sustain a behavior change if it is not aligned with how you see yourself. *Psycho-Cybernetics* by Maxwell Maltz is often cited as the preeminent book explaining the mind, body, results connection. Further studies across a wide variety of disciplines have confirmed the impact the mind has on results.

Therefore, when you want to change anything in your life, address your beliefs. If you do not tackle your limiting beliefs first, you will struggle to make lasting changes. Or, in the words of James Allen, you will "remain bound."

STARTING YOUR STRENGTH BUILDING JOURNEY

Could you run a marathon tomorrow? Your answer may be yes if you have been training for it. Alternatively, your answer may be, "Not today, but I could if I trained and built my strength."
Knowing you can do something, like run a marathon if given the right tools and training, is a big step towards developing the strength of belief and action required to achieve your success.

Awareness is the first step needed to implement change. Owning your belief is the second step. Acting is the third. Over time, taking that action repeatedly creates a habit that supports your new belief—the fourth step of change.

1. Awareness

2. Ownership
3. Action
4. Habit

Awareness first means you have knowledge that something exists. As your awareness or knowledge of something deepens, it includes understanding how you are related to it. When you become more aware of your life, you will notice you are at different levels of awareness in different areas of your life. As your awareness of your beliefs grows, you will see where you need to take ownership and action to make improvements.

Ownership of your beliefs, and the results they have produced in your life, is a critical step in changing them. Take time to examine your beliefs. Then own them, no matter how helpful or unhelpful they may be. Only when you own your beliefs can you challenge and change them. Or in other words, take action to create new habits that build your new identity. You can't be a victim and have ownership. Nothing changes without action. Habits become your companion and define who you are. You can change direction with one turn, but it requires consistent habitual action to travel any distance. Every time you repeat the four-step change process, the compound effect kicks in—building your strength, affirming your new identity, and taking you to a new level of success.

As you move forward, you will slip and fall. That's normal. Don't panic. Take a deep breath and keep moving. The key is to give yourself grace as you grow. You are learning to be a new, stronger expression of yourself and how to keep going despite setbacks. You're building strength, and from strength comes resiliency.

EXERCISE

1. Write three things you believe to be true about yourself.

   _____
   _____
   _____

2. Examine your list. Ask yourself how these beliefs support who you want to become.

_____
_____
_____
_____

3. What actions can you take to build those beliefs that support your future self?

_____
_____
_____
_____

NOURISHING YOUR STRENGTH

In the chapter titled Overcoming the Darkness, I introduced the idea of nutrition and told you that we would come back to it.

Nourish means providing your body with the substances necessary for growth. Nourish also means feeding your beliefs in a way that offers growth. I want to share with you the power of good nutrition to nourish your life and strength—physically, mentally, and emotionally.

I read a story about the ancient world of kings and prophets, camels, and battles. The hero was an outspoken leader of his people and challenged the self-serving political leaders of his day. In the story, the political tension had come to a dramatic face-off against the many, and the hero won. Pure blockbuster movie material! What happened next in the story was most telling. There was no victory celebration, no awards, no dinners, no speaking engagements—nothing like that.

Why not? After all, the hero had won the battle. The hero should have been given a position of honor and a few thousand likes on his social media feed, or the equivalent for his time. Instead, the hero ended up alone in the wilderness—worn out, depressed, scared for his life. The hero cried out, "God, I've always done the right thing. I've put up with so much. I've done so much. I'm the only one left who will stand up for what's right, and they are trying to kill me! It's not fair!" He received his answer in the form of an angel telling him, "Sleep, drink, and eat." The angel repeated the instructions: "Sleep, drink, eat." Then the hero was told why. "Sleep, get up and eat, or the journey will be too much for you."

After any battle, through any journey, we need to care for ourselves. Good sleep and nourishing food are not optional on your success journey. If you want success, sleep well, then "get up and eat, or the journey will be too much for you."

That sleep, food, and drink gave our hero enough strength to travel for an additional forty days. Not forever, but just enough to arrive at the next place on his journey. This new place was a place of reflection, healing, and, again, sleep. This time, the hero came to a place where his mental, emotional, and spiritual vision was fed and renewed, as well as his physical body.

In terms of his journey, the hero came to a place where he needed to make a new start. To start anew, he had to slow down, reflect, and prepare. Once he discovered what he needed and was rested, nourished, and ready physically and mentally for his next task, he started forward again.

During the hero's time of reflection and renewal, he became aware he was not alone. Others supported his cause. Our hero gained new clarity and direction and knew what to do next. He sought team members to take the journey with him. He realized he didn't need to do it all on his own any longer.

Being the lone individual may make a good movie, but it never makes for great reality. If you look carefully, behind every hero, you will see there is a team that helps the hero on their quest. You need a team that can help you stay on your path in good and bad times. Finding your team will require you to slow down long enough to decide: 1. the strengths and talent you will need on your team, and 2. to look around you and find them. The people you need are there. You just need to realize them and ask them to join you.

These questions may help you develop your team.

EXERCISE

1. List three people who most inspire you.

   _____

   _____

   _____

2. What is it about them that inspires you?

   _____

   _____

   _____

   _____

When you have answered the above, ask the people you have listed if they would be willing to support you on your journey. If they can't help you, ask them to recommend people who can.

SUMMARY

- Building strength allows you to face and deal with life's challenges.
- Strength is not static. You can grow your strength every day.
- Identity, beliefs, thoughts, actions, and results are linked and can be strengthened.
- When you change your beliefs, you potentially change everything.
- Beliefs drive thinking.
- Thinking drives action.
- Actions create habits.
- Your habits create your results.
- Nourish your body and mind so you have strength for your journey.
- Sleep and food are necessary, not optional extras.

Chapter 7
Feeding Your Tomorrows

"All the flowers of tomorrow are in the seeds of today."
Robin Craig Clark

Who you can be and what you can achieve tomorrow starts with who you are and what you do today? What you plant today, you can harvest in the future. No planting, no harvest. It is also said, "What you feed grows!" It's not what you occasionally feed that grows to change your life. It is what you feed daily that grows to become your life.

So how do you improve your tomorrow today? You feed your mind and build your capacity by learning today with the focus on who you want to become tomorrow.

You start by learning. If you feel a need to change but don't know how, ask yourself if you could change one thing in your life, what would it be. When you have focused on one change you wish to make, you can look at how are you are feeding the negative results you don't want and stop the thinking and actions that are feeding the unwanted results. You can then feed the thinking and actions that will produce the results you are looking to achieve.

Sometimes the thinking that needs to change is a learned mindset. Think of a defining experience in your life. What lessons did you learn from the experience? Positive, negative? Are those lessons supporting your success today or holding you back? How can you apply a different mindset to that situation and change the lessons learned? Check your mindset. Choose and feed a growth mindset.

Your journey will require you to learn new things, and there is more than one way to learn. When you learned to drive a car, you were likely already familiar with driving by watching others drive. This is an example of observational learning. However, when it came time to get behind the wheel, a different type of learning was required—experiential learning. Experiential learning works best in a safe but challenging environment.

When I learned to drive, my parents signed me up with the local driving school. They wanted me to be taught by someone who had experience teaching driving. My driving lessons started on a simulator, a safe but still challenging environment. The simulator was not reality but helped me develop the skills I needed to face the reality of the busy roads.

When I wanted to learn to fly an airplane, a different level of learning altogether was required. With no prior observational learning to draw from, the instructor started everyone in a small group in the classroom, building flight awareness.

After completing the classroom training, during which the rules and risks were explained, the instructor took the class out onto the tarmac. Once on the tarmac, the "good manners" and safety lessons were repeated while walking around a parked airplane.

Those early classroom lessons built awareness and provided knowledge that not only kept us safe but also kept everybody else safe from us! The first lessons were basic things like, "This is a propeller," and "This is a wing. Only walk on these specially marked areas, or you will damage what holds you in the air." These lessons might seem overly simple, but the reality is when we start with the basics, we develop a firm foundation for success.

LEARNING NEW SKILLS AND HABITS

When you develop new skills, you open yourself to new horizons and opportunities. Some skills you learn will become habits and part of your everyday life.

As a trainee pilot, there were many new skills to be learned. After checking the flight worthiness of the aircraft, the next skill to learn was how to taxi.

- Step one: learn the mechanics of taxiing.
- Step two: taxi from where I was parked to where I would take off.

Seems simple enough. You would be amazed at how many details I had to learn between walking out to the aircraft, getting into the aircraft, starting the aircraft, and moving the aircraft from one location to the next. The thing is, when you start something new, the steps of moving from no knowledge to a little knowledge can be quite steep.

The aircraft I trained in had dual controls so the instructor could take control of the plane at any moment. This allowed me to feel safe while I focused on mastering a new skill. The first skill was taxiing. I learned that taxiing is not flying, but you will never get off the ground until you learn to do it well. In the beginning, taxiing was exhausting because there was so much to think about, so many details to concentrate on. But slowly, over time, the conscious actions became unconscious actions. When that happened, I could free my mind to focus on mastering the next skill required.

UNLEARNING AND LEARNING

When you pilot a plane, you don't just have a conversation. Cockpit communication comes with new rules and requires new skills. I had to pass my radio operator's license before even starting in the aircraft! You could say I had to learn to talk airplane talk before learning airplane walk.

In the beginning, with all the noise of the aircraft, I could barely hear or understand the radio messages. As I spent more time learning what to listen for, it became easier. When I didn't understand what was said, the required response was, "Say again." Sometimes the air traffic controllers may not have heard or understood my message. "Say again" would come across the radio from the control tower until a mutual understanding was achieved.

I even had to learn a new alphabet. A was not A; it was Alpha. To make learning fast, I created a game using license plates. Every time a car passed me on the road, I would read out the license plate in radio speech. *Alpha, Bravo, Charlie…*

Aviation communication wasn't easy at first. I made many mistakes and had to "say again" often. It took longer than I wanted, but I persevered and succeeded. What was hard and tiring at first became easy.

But that's the way it goes. When you first learned a new skill, you probably felt exhausted from the sheer concentration of learning. After mastering the skill, much of what you had to think about consciously became routine or an unconscious habit. Remember, making changes to create your success will feel exhausting at first. Keep going.

When preparing for your success, it's not only about learning and mastering new skills but also about stopping some of the automatic responses that are blocking you. To do this, you need to make the unconscious habits conscious again so you can examine them, improve them, or replace them. It will be like me having to learn to communicate all over again.

Are you prepared to go back to basics, learn new skills, make mistakes, fail, get back up, and fail again all to succeed? In his book *The Slight Edge*, author Jeff Olson calls this process "mastering the mundane." He says, "The truth is, what you do matters. What you do today matters. What you do every day matters." This is another way of saying, "What you feed grows."

Learning to master the mundane was perhaps my greatest lesson from those initial flying lessons. What first felt so difficult became routine. Flying also taught me that when you master the mundane in one area of your life, that mastery will often flow into other areas of your life and open new horizons and opportunities. "Whatever good things we build end up building us," was a favorite teaching of Dr. Jim Rohn. Build good into the mundane of life, and you will build a good life.

EXERCISE

1. What new skills will help you go toward your success?

_____

_____

_____

_____

2. When will you start learning your new skill?

_____

_____

_____

_____

3. What do you want to and need to change in your life?

_____

_____

_____

_____

4. What action will you take this week to achieve that?

_____

_____

_____

_____

ENERGIZING YOUR FUTURE

How enthusiastic or energetic do you feel about your future? Do you feel your energy level increasing or decreasing? Energy is not something you have or don't have, and therefore you are stuck. Energy is something you create. You are like a power plant. From the raw materials of your life, you create energy. If you want more energy, like a fire, you need to add more fuel.

What fuels your energy and your success? When you make changes, you will spend more time feeding the process of change than seeing results, as results may not be immediate. Even new logs on a fire take time to catch and burn. For a fire to warm the house, you will need to keep stoking the fire by adding more fuel. Because change takes time to see, you can easily be tempted to forget that truth and think, "Nothing's happening. It's not making any difference. I'll stop." Keep feeding what creates the energy required to fuel your success.

KEEP ON TRACK

A question I am often asked is, "How do you know things are improving if you can't see change?" You make progress visible by measuring it. At first, you may track your consistent actions and direction. A simple system to track how you shift your energy is to give yourself a score for your overall energy for the day. When you do that daily for a week, you will see a pattern. Today you may feel your score is seven versus yesterday when you felt like a four. You will see a shift if you can hold yourself accountable and track your energy for a week. When you use the information to understand what drives your energy level up and what pulls it down, you can take action to move into operating with a higher energy state.

FEEDING YOUR TOMORROW TODAY

Maybe you have been like the hero in my earlier story, fighting battles without taking time to pause, feed, sleep, and renew. If so, give yourself permission to take time to pause, rest, and nourish yourself so you can prepare and start again. I have a simple three-step process that helps me recharge, keep my energy high, and create a life full of joy.

1. Good In – I look for the excellent fuel in the things I eat, the books I read, the thoughts I think, the people I am around, and the words I let into my mind.
2. Bad Out – On the opposite side, I look for the bad fuel in my life and then chuck it.
3. Exercise for Strength – Practice daily the habits that build my health, mindset, values, and beliefs.

This restart process is supported by three simple questions and three deeper questions I ask myself about the choices I'm making or the actions I'm taking.

Three Simple Questions:
1. Is this choice in line with my values and my goals?
2. If I do this, how will I feel in one hour, one day, one week?
3. What will the long-term outcome be if I do this consistently?

Three Deeper Questions:
1. Will this choice increase or diminish my physical, mental, and spiritual energy?
2. Will this choice help me become the best version of myself that I can be today?
3. Will this choice lead me towards or away from my dreams?

When I take time to slow down and ask myself these questions, it helps me decide, "Will I do this or not?" or "Is there a better option?"

As I shared at the beginning of this chapter, "All the flowers of your tomorrow are in the seeds of your today." The choices you make today become and energize your tomorrow.

SUMMARY

- Who you can be and what you can achieve tomorrow starts with what you do today.
- What you feed grows.
- It's what you do daily that will change your life.
- Start by learning.
- Master the mundane.
- Make room for new ideas by getting rid of old ones that do not serve you.
- Make your unconscious habits conscious and improve them.
- Track your energy.
- Fill your energy fuel tank.
- Healthy Body, Mind, Spirit Checklist:
    - Good In
    - Bad Out
    - Exercise for Strength
- Plant seeds today for a harvest tomorrow.

Chapter 8

Measuring and Tracking Your Progress

"One accurate measurement is worth one thousand expert opinions."
Grace Hopper

This is the final chapter in Section 2 as you get set for your journey. I want to take a moment and say WELL DONE! You have grown so much. I know you have achieved much already, even though it may not feel like it. That is often the case when you first start out.

What you measure, you manage; and what you manage, you control. I can see some of you rolling your eyes at hearing the word "measure." Maybe you have experienced situations where there were many measurements and compliance issues to track, and you didn't have the time or energy to do the work. I understand. I worked in government and have seen this situation far too many times. I don't want you to do that to yourself. Measure, yes, but don't overcomplicate things.

With a flight plan, the pilot continually measures his position against the planned route. Knowing where they are, combined with a few other key measurements, helps the pilot to navigate the weather, adjust the flight course, and arrive safely at the destination. Systems and simple checklists help the pilot succeed, and they will also help you as you navigate your success.

A measure is taken using an instrument or device marked in standard units. It can be inches and centimeters on a ruler or a complex scientific tool. The secret is to use the right instrument that supports what you are trying to measure and track. A Fitbit will provide measures that support your activity goals but not your eating habits. Measuring spoons and cups will help you measure your eating habits but not your activity level. But what measures will help you on your journey to success?

To choose the right measures for you, consider two main points:
1. Your situation
2. What you desire to achieve

Then choose your measures to help you achieve the result without being a burden. Do only what will support you to achieve your desired outcome. What you decide to measure and track may look very different from what I or your parent, friend, or colleague chooses. Borrow ideas that work for you, but don't slavishly copy others. Measure, track, reflect, and course-correct in ways that support you, your journey, your environment, and the life you choose to live.

To achieve success, don't just measure once, then forget. Track. True tracking is about gauging the results over time. By tracking, you can validate your results, change your actions, or improve how you measure. Tracking improves outcomes and allows course-correction as required.

The Success Measurement Process I use is:
1. Measure
2. Track
3. Reflect
4. Course-Correct

The best measures for life and success are journey measures. Journey measures track where you were, where you're at, and where you're going. These measurements will let you know where you are and track the distance covered.

To know which measures are best for you, ask yourself:
- What is the most important change I want to see?
- What measure supports that change?
- What will encourage me to track over time?

When you have answered these questions, choose what you will measure and how you will measure it. Then check your chosen measures against the lists below. If they pass the useful measure checklist, start and continue measuring!

Useful Measure Checklist

Measure

- Know why you are measuring
- Measure what you care about
- Use simple, clear measures when possible
- Measure what drives your success
- Only measure what makes sense and supports the outcomes you seek

Don't measure…

- What you don't care about or is unimportant
- Too many measures; avoid creating overwhelm, and don't let important measures get lost
- What is easy to measure but doesn't drive your success

Track measurements to…

- Know where you are
- Know when you are on or off course
- Know when and how you can course-correct

In *The Lord of the Rings*, "one ring ruled them all." In developing measurements, there is also one measure that rules them all—The Key Performance Measure! It is said Lord King turned around the performance and culture of British Airways using one measure—on-time flight departure.

Another personal favorite example of choosing a great key performance measure is from a North American business owner. The company was large, covering multiple locations in multiple states. Profits at this company were stalling, so the business owner spent more and more time traveling from location to location, trying to fix things. This business was his dream, but he was thinking of selling out with all the problems now. In the midst of all that was happening, the owner realized he had lost his love for his business.

Before deciding to sell the company, he paused and reflected on what had changed over the years. He also reassessed what was important for him in this new season of his business. He realized the core problem he faced was he loved spending time with his family, and business was taking him away from them. Having to spend so many days on the road was draining his energy and love for the business.

With this new understanding, he talked with his wife, and together, they devised a new business key performance measure (KPM) based on the number of nights he would be home each year to tuck his young son into bed.

The company still kept the usual measures. However, the owner shifted his focus for his personal "tuck-son-into-bed" KPM. Shifting his KPM worked for him and the company because the addition of this personal priority resulted in increased energy and love for his business again. This creative, non-financial measure resulted in national expansion and multi-million dollar increases to the company's financial bottom line over the next two years!

When the business owner did the "importance" self-check, he discovered that family was key for him. Only with that knowledge could he choose and set a personally appropriate measure that supported his success, not only for his family but also for his business.

What personal measures should you take, and what changes would support your success? Take a moment and be creative!

MEASURING UP, DOWN, AND ALL AROUND

I am a big picture person. I can get lost with too many details, yet I still need enough details to balance conflicting priorities. So, I created a visual tool to help me. This tool looks like a star with five points. It is my star map, and it reminds me to act and measure across all five key areas of my life and effectively prioritize them. This process became my *Be a Star* program.

EXERCISE

1. What are the five most important areas in your life?

   _____

   _____

   _____

   _____

2. Describe what success looks like for each area.

_____

_____

_____

_____

3. Create a measure that will help you drive your success in each area.

_____

_____

_____

_____

GETTING ON TRACK WITH JOY

High energy levels are one of the best predictors of success. And one of the best drivers of energy is joy!

One of my all-time favorite quotes is, *"I believe a joyful life is made up of joyful moments gracefully strung together by trust, gratitude, inspiration, and faith."* by Brene Brown.

Joyful moments strung together! Trust. Gratitude. Inspiration. Faith. I can create my joyful moments and create a more joyful life. So can you. Because joy and energy go together, you can shift your energy and joy—moment by moment, step by step—creating and navigating your success.

Research has shown that you will create more joy when you track joy in your life. Also, when something is enjoyable, it is easier to repeat and therefore easier to develop strong habits that serve you well. Therefore, to bring more energy and joy to your life, look for ways to create fun.

Don't get me wrong, not everything you have to do to achieve your goals and dreams will be fun. There will always be parts of your journey that are hard work, like climbing a mountain. Some aspects you may even dislike. I don't always like getting up at five a.m. to go walking, particularly when it is minus five degrees Celsius. It is tempting to give in and say I'll go tomorrow. But I know I do enjoy the beautiful walk around the lake with my husband. And I feel energized when I have finished walking. Coffee with my husband afterwards at our favorite café makes it an even more special experience. Tracking the action keeps me motivated and increases my success.

EXERCISE

1. What can you do to create an extra joyful moment in your life every day this week?

_____

_____

_____

_____

KEEPING ON TRACK

It is important to consistently check that the measures you are using are in alignment and producing the results intended. After my initial flying lessons, learning navigation became a priority. The skill of navigation includes many sub-skills, such as map reading, creating a flight plan, course plotting, and vectoring for wind and weather, to name a few. Each skill required new measures!

My first big cross-country flight was a whole day event. First task, receive weather reports and plot the course. Then five hours of flying—one stop and two directional changes at specific towns. Lunch was at a small country town airport en route to my destination. That was a special treat. Visiting pilots could make a cup of tea or coffee and buy and cook a piece of steak! Steak sandwich for lunch. Yum.

Over lunch, I checked the updated weather report and adjusted the flight plan accordingly. We took off, and I flew the headings as per the flight plan. However, the features on the ground did not match what I expected from the map. I took my bearings. My instructor was talking on the radio, so I couldn't hear! Things seemed very suspicious.

"Do you know where you are? Are you lost?" he asked.

I worked out that I was not on the planned flight path. I was off course. After looking around a little longer and taking my bearings in alignment with the map, I told the instructor where I thought I was. I was very close, but I was off course from the intended route. I didn't know why, but I found out.

I had set and measured direction using a gyroscope. Gyroscopes need to be regularly reset to the compass. In my case, the compass and gyroscope were not aligned, so what I was measuring was taking me off course! I took the time to reset the gyroscope back in alignment with the compass and completed a mid-flight course-correction. Soon, I was back on track, heading home.

The lessons I learned that day have helped me intentionally guide my life ever since.

- Measure what is important to stay on track.
- Check your alignment.
- Track against your planned course.
- Observe continually.
- Know where you are.

I realized if you don't measure what you need to know, you won't be able to course-correct to navigate for your success. Like my gyroscope and compass, if you are out of alignment with who you are and what is important to you, your life will be out of alignment, and you won't arrive where you want to go.

EXERCISE

1. What can you do to experience greater alignment?

_____

_____

_____

2. What measurements will help you know your position, progress, and support you to course-correct?

_____

_____

_____

_____

TURNING EXPERIENCE INTO GUIDEPOSTS

When you plan a big trip, do you create a checklist to help you prepare? Checklists can be invaluable. As well as measuring and tracking your progress, you can support your success through checklists that act as guideposts to keep you on track. You can find checklists online that help you, or you can create your own. Think of your past successes. Your experiences can be written down and used to create a guide for further success.

Previously I shared how taking DISC Personality Assessments and training helped my husband and I better understand ourselves, each other, and our family. Reflecting on our process, I wrote down the steps and adapted them to create a checklist.

You can take your success process and create your personal success checklist! Checklists can be in a statement or question format. I created this checklist reflecting on a communication learning experience with my husband that went extremely well. I started with a description of the experience and then turned the statements into questions I could use as a checklist in future experiences.

Relationship Situation Checklist

☐ Can I describe what is happening in this situation?
☐ Do I understand why this is happening?
☐ Do I understand what I'm feeling and own my emotions?
☐ Can I clearly explain what is important for me and why?
☐ Am I/Are we communicating in a non-judgmental way to create understanding?
☐ Do I understand what the others believe about this situation?
☐ Do I understand the other parties' emotions in this situation?

- ☐ Do I understand what is important for them and why?
- ☐ Are we celebrating each other's uniqueness?
- ☐ Do all parties know what each other stands for and what we seek to achieve together?
- ☐ Together, can we examine all options and find the best way forward?

EXERCISE

Write out one of your own learning experiences and create a checklist?

_____

_____

_____

_____

You are now prepared and equipped to step outside your comfort zone and create your success daily as you navigate your success journey. Section Three will take you there.

SUMMARY

- Measure to know where you are and how far you have come.
- Measure what you care about.
- Measure only what supports you and your journey.
- Measure enough but not too much.
- Make your reality more joyful by making more joyful moments.
- Track energy in your life, and you will create more energy.
- Track joy in your life, and you will create more joy.
- Create your own best practice processes and checklists.

START

Chapter 9

Connecting with Your World

"Connection is why we are here. It gives purpose and meaning to our lives."
Brene Brown

So far, we have covered the READY and SET. Now let's move into the START section of this book. As you step out into your journey, it will always start with making connections. Connecting is an action word meaning linking or bringing together. That is why connection is the perfect word to describe a relationship. We are forming connections all the time. Our lives become a web of connections to places, people, ideas, dreams, events, and goals.

These connections do several things. First, they help us see gain perspective, and second, they open doors for us. Third, connection allows us to interact with our world—to change it and be changed by it to break the isolation. Connections also create a sense of belonging and break the boredom of life. If you were to examine the connections in your life and the influence these connections have over your actions and decisions that ultimately lead to your success, you would understand why this lesson is the first we discuss as we move into the big world of our journey.

CONNECTING FOR LIFE

Dean Ornish, a physician, researcher, and Clinical Professor of Medicine at the University of California, San Francisco, says, "The need for connection and community is primal and as fundamental as the need for air, water, and food." The need for connection is not only a fundamental physical need, but it also brings meaning and purpose to our lives. Without connections, there is no life, no power. It is well documented that a baby that fails to connect will fail to thrive, and if the lack of physical connection goes on too long, the infant will die.

You can only prevail in achieving your success if you are alive and thriving. To be alive and thriving requires strong, positive connections. Therefore, to succeed on your terms in your way, you need to establish four types of connections intentionally.

1. Connection to self.
2. Connection to others.
3. Connection to your hopes and dreams.
4. Connection to your world.

EXERCISE

Take a moment and write out the three most powerful connections you have to people, places, habits, or beliefs.-

_____

_____

_____

CONNECTING WITH SELF

Let's take a moment and talk about connecting to self. It may seem strange to talk about having to intentionally connect with ourselves, especially after I said connecting requires two or more people or objects. However, connecting to self means knowing who you are and what you stand for at the deepest level. When you are connected to self, your thoughts, words, and actions match. Think of connecting to self as the alignment of your many parts—head, heart, soul, and actions. Like the coming together of cars on a train, they form a single train and move in one direction.

 Clear connections allow us to make clear choices, and choices are the only thing we really control in life. Your choices drive your actions and habits, ultimately giving you energy and filling you with peace and joy. With no connection to yourself, there is no peace, power, or joy.

Connecting to yourself is not a one-time event. You will have to connect and reconnect over and over on your success journey. One way you can tell if you're positively connected to yourself is when you can define what success means to you for every area of your life, in line with your most deeply held values.

So how do you connect to self? You start the connection process by becoming curious and honest with yourself. Become an explorer of who you are and what you believe. When you develop a growth mindset, you put on your explorer hat and ask yourself questions, realize who you are, and become accountable for acting.

The fear most people have is what if you don't like what you find out about yourself-as you go through the process of being curious and honest. While you are in this process, try to avoid self-judgment. Give yourself some grace. Don't feel a need to put a positive or negative on what you discover. Instead, seek just to understand. Beating yourself up for not being good enough or what you "could've, would've, should've" done is not helpful. The fact is, judgment is the death of growth and causes loss of connection to the truth you seek.

Connecting with yourself is just the beginning. By building a strong alignment with yourself, you can build stronger connections with others and the world around you.

- Connection to yourself is the foundation of your success.
- Connection to yourself develops self-acceptance.
- Self-acceptance fuels a sense of true belonging.
- True belonging is the foundation to positively connecting with others.
- Connecting with others empowers your hopes and dreams.
- Living out your hopes and dreams connects you with your world and drives your life and contribution to the world.
- The actions of your daily life and the contribution you make to the world are your success.

EXERCISE

1. When you are connected to self, your energy and joy increase. Finish the sentence: I have the most energy and feel most joyful when...

_____

_____

_____

2. Where do I need to dig deeper and build a stronger connection to myself?

_____

_____

_____

_____

CONNECTING TO OTHERS

Connecting with others can be fun, and sometimes it can be scary! As much as some of us want to act like we live on an island, we don't. So, we need to accept that we must be among other people. We will always be required to connect to others, whether at work, at home, or in the community. You will always touch the lives of others, and others will touch yours—every single day.

The good news is connecting to others is a skill that can be learned and developed. The more you master the skill of connection to others, the stronger the connections will become. Your attitude, character, and level of interest in others will affect your ability to create those interpersonal connections. That is why your choices about who you are and what you stand for strongly affect your ability to connect with others.

The idea of connection and belonging goes hand in hand, says Brene Brown. Her research showed, "We are biologically, cognitively, physically, and spiritually wired to love, be loved, and belong," and "True belonging only happens when we present our authentic, imperfect selves to the world." Your sense of belonging can never be greater than your level of self-acceptance. That is why we started with connection to self.

The greater your connections–the greater your life–the greater your success!

So, how do you develop a strong connection with others? You choose a growth mindset, a positive attitude; you learn new skills; you strengthen your character and cultivate your interest in others and your world.

Connection requires strong communication skills. Listening skills are part of that commutation skill set and a great place to start. If you want to develop your listening skills, do the following:

- Listen to understand, not just respond.
- Ask questions to clarify understanding.
- Reflect on what you think you heard until understanding is reached.

Your character plays a huge role in whom and how you connect to others. You are attracted to people and organizations with similar qualities and values. To strengthen your character, ask yourself the following:

- What are your strongest character qualities?
- What qualities would you like to develop?
- Do you live your values daily?
- Trust is the key. Being trustworthy is key to building trust in relationships.

By cultivating common interests, you more naturally connect with others. Join groups where you can meet others who share your interests. Also, reach out and participate in different groups to learn about new ideas and try new activities.

- What are your interests?
- How aware are you of what's happening around you?
- Know what you care about and value.
- You attract who you are.

EXERCISE

Choose three things you will do to develop your mindset, attitude, skills, character, and interests.

_____

_____

_____

CONNECTING WITH YOUR HOPES AND DREAMS

We all have hopes and dreams. Maybe you have stopped chasing your dreams because holding on to hope for those dreams was too painful. Guess what? You can restart living in your dream anytime.

I have been asked so often, "Is dreaming dreams and setting goals worth it?" My answer is, "In life, you always have a choice to do something or nothing." When answering the "worth it" question, I ask myself, "Am I worth it? Is my family, health, or future worth it?" So, I ask you, "Are you worth it? Is your family worth it? Is your health worth it? Is your future worth it?"

If you are looking to start your dreams and goals, start by asking, "What is worth it?" and "Who is worth it?" When you answer these questions, you will find your *why*. That "why" is the seed to your dreams. And you, too, will say yes to the "worth it" question! When you find your *why*, you find your way.

I want you to know connecting to your hopes and dreams is not fast or easy! My experiences have taught me that my hopes and dreams will take longer, be harder, and work out differently than what I first expected. But connecting to and pursuing your dreams and goals is absolutely worth it. Think about it; if you could easily achieve your dream without growth or help, it wouldn't be much of a dream, would it? Your dreams are always greater than your current abilities. That's why they are called goals or dreams. Being deeply connected to them provides the power to persist through the challenges and struggles you will face to become someone who can achieve and live your dream.

CONNECTING WITH YOUR WORLD

There is a bigger world out there than you currently know. To connect with your world, you must first become aware of what makes up your world. If you ignore your environment or take it for granted, you do so to your peril. Your environment feeds you, provides the stage for your life, and contributes to your success. When you find yourself in a toxic environment, you have two choices: stay and work to change your environment, or leave to find a healthier environment that is more conducive to your success.

Starting your journey, stepping out your front door can be both fun and scary. As you start your journey of success, you will connect to and interact with every environment and type of situation you can imagine and then some.

Perhaps you might feel a little like Frodo in J. R. R. Tolkien's novel, *The Hobbit*, when Bilbo told him, "It's a dangerous business, Frodo, going out the door. You step onto the road, and if you don't keep your feet, there's no knowing where you might be swept off to."

If stepping out seems scary, ask yourself what the dangers are of not stepping out. What are the dangers of staying put, doing nothing, and staying scared? Jim Rohn said, "The difficulties you meet will resolve themselves as you advance. Proceed, and the light will dawn and shine with increasing clearness on your path!"

Fear can block positive connections. Fear can also lead to negative and toxic connections. If you allow fear to overtake you, you will lose opportunities and your hope. You may even lose your newfound sense of self. When starting out, much of the fear centers around not knowing what will happen, not knowing what to expect. Learn to allow for the unexpected. It is unrealistic to think that everything will work out perfectly the first time. Be bold. Don't wait in fear. Instead, expect the unexpected, but do not fear it. The safety of the known is a false illusion. As Jim Rohn said, the difficulties you meet will resolve themselves as you advance. Leave your fear mindset behind.

Choose an adventure mindset. Choose courage. When you do so, your unexpected moments will still bring challenges, but joy and new opportunities will arise in those challenges.

EXERCISE

What actions will you take to face your fears and step out?

_____

_____

_____

_____

CONNECTING CREATES RIPPLES

The connections you create will affect the person you become, where you will go, and how you will experience the road ahead. These connections will create ripples beyond you.

In 1962, a book, *Silent Spring*, was published that created a huge ripple. To date, *Silent Spring* has been through multiple editions and is still in publication. The book was, above all, about the interconnectedness of life and the ripples that flow from that interconnection. The author, Rachel Carson, wanted to make the world a safer place by showing the impact and interconnection of man and the environment. "*Silent Spring* translated the central truth of ecology that everything in nature is related to everything else," wrote the commentator, Linda Lear. Through her research, Rachel Carson outlined the process and power of this interconnection. For perhaps the first time, our interconnection with our physical world was seen and understood. The truth being, we are in an inter-dependent relationship with our physical world, like it or not.

Silent Spring documented not only how this interconnectedness brought life but contained a warning about how the creation of a toxic environment would bring environmental death and place human life in danger of self-destruction.

Your environment is critical to your success. A healthy environment feeds you, molds you, and provides the canvas for your contribution. Your connection to the environment can be positive and life-giving or negative and destructive. You choose.

5 Steps to Connect Positively:

1. Connect with your world.
2. Remain true to yourself.
3. Hone your skills.
4. Speak up.
5. Pay the price.

CONNECTING COSTS

Whatever you do, there are always costs as well as potential benefits. Not all costs are monetary. The costs may also be energy, time, emotional, mental, or physical. Rachel Carson's story shows all five steps to a positive connection. Ms. Carson paid a considerable price when she published *Silent Spring*. The corporations, whose income was threatened by the revelations she shared in the book, sought to stop publication. When that failed, they attacked the messenger and denigrated the message. Until her death, Rachel Carson continually had to pay a cost for doing what she believed was right and speaking out for the truth. Because of her passion, she never gave up fighting to bring awareness of the power and responsibility of interconnectedness.

Understand that every journey has a cost. You will always pay for what you do or don't do. By answering the cost question upfront, your connections will become more in alignment with whom you are and what you stand for. Stop paying the price, and you stop progressing.

You will always pay a cost, but you can still manage your expenses. Some expenses are just that. Other costs become an investment in yourself and your future. You choose if your cost is an expense or an investment. Start choosing to manage your cost by ensuring you are investing in creating your future.

Have you ever bought something and later thought, "I wish I hadn't bought that" or "I paid too much"? Yes, there might come a time when the price is too high for the reward. When you have sorted the cost question, you will know what is important and why, and you will never pay too much again.

EXERCISE
Create two lists.
1. The first list will outline what price you are willing to pay for your success.
2. The second list will outline what you will not pay.

You can use the list below to prompt your thinking. Note, these are about relative importance and priorities. Your answers will differ from others. Don't worry. There is no right or wrong answer. It is what is right for you and your definition of success.

- Relationships - If you lose your friends, family, partners along the way, would it be worth it?
- Time - Time is critical. You cannot make more. How much will you invest?
- Health - To what degree are you willing to risk your current or future health?
- Energy - How will you use the limited resource of your energy? Are you willing to work to the point of exhaustion? If so, for what

cause?
- Values & Integrity - Will you sacrifice your values, lose trust, self-integrity? Others have to achieve a dream. Will you?
- Home - Will you give up the comfort of home? Will you move, live apart, become a nomad? Risk your home?
- Money - How will you allocate money? What is the "no turning back" point for you financially? Are you willing to sell everything for your dream?
- Life - Are you prepared to pay with your life?

_____

_____

_____

_____

CONNECTING FOR SUCCESS

Rachel Carson lived what she cared deeply about, and because of that, her life affected the world for the better. Her journey to success led her to grow beyond author to become a person of influence, a leader. Your journey will require you to start, grow, persist, face obstacles, and become the person who can contribute to your world in your unique way.

I shared the lessons from Ms. Carson's journey to show how journeys start with a vision, and when that vision is strong and clear, it can become your life. When that happens and your journey aligns with whom you are, you will hold on to your vision and pay the price required to see it through.

SUMMARY

- Connection creates relationships.
- Connection with your world allows you to navigate it and change it.
- Connection is a source of life.
- Four areas of connection
    1. Self
    2. Others
    3. Your hopes and dreams

-
    4. Your environment
- The ecology of life, everything in life is connected.
- Your world needs you
    1. Connect with your world
    2. Remain true to yourself
    3. Hone your skills
    4. Speak up
    5. Pay the price
- Everything has a cost.
- The cost can be emotional, physical, relational, financial, spiritual, and even life itself.
- When you stop paying the cost, you stop progressing.

Chapter 10
Navigating Your Life

"A map does not just chart, it unlocks and formulates meaning; it forms bridges between here and there, between disparate ideas that we did not know were previously connected."
Reif Larsen

Now that you have stepped out and connected to the big world, how do you successfully navigate and create success? Which way do you go? Today you hear of navigating ships, cars, airplanes, even spaceships. In our world of high-tech self-guiding navigation, it would be easy to think navigating your life is as simple as plugging in, powering up, and sitting back. But it is not that simple. To direct the course of your journey of success, you need to navigate, which requires intentional thinking and action, skills, and tools.

Navigation presupposes that you are going somewhere. If you don't have a destination or direction in mind or are not actively navigating your life, you are at the mercy of whatever forces are around you, even when standing still. Learning navigation skills will empower you to choose your direction, plot your course, and successfully navigate your journey to success.

In chapter one, you read about my climb up Mount Kinabalu in Borneo to see the sunrise. I knew which way to go—up! But I didn't *know* the way. There was a path, but the path disappeared at several points over rocks and small cliff faces. So, I had a guide to help me find the way. If I had been left to explore on my own, I would not have made the summit by sunrise. I would not have achieved my goal.

In the summer, my daughter and I love walking together in the rugged high country of the Snowy Mountains. J. R. R. Tolkien said, "Not all who wander are lost." Sometimes we walk to wander and explore—no specific destination, just a general direction and timeframe. But even for a wander, we go prepared—carrying water, food, and protective gear as the weather can change quickly. Snow, rain, and strong winds can quickly turn a hot sunny day into a freezing, life-threatening experience.

Other times, we plan hikes to specific locations. Mount Kosciusko, Australia's highest mountain, is a favorite destination. For some of these walks, we can follow marked tracks. The paths may be wide and relatively smooth or winding and rugged. Often, they are a mix of both. But often, we walk cross-country, where there are no paths. We make our own. To do this requires a higher level of navigation and preparation. We carry communication beacons and food, water, and foul weather gear. We plan our route, then notify others of our intentions and expected return. We use a map and compass to determine our course and a watch to track time against our position as we walk. With those instruments, we can set direction, know we are on track or if we need to change our course, and successfully complete our journey.

NAVIGATING MADE SIMPLE

Three keys that help you navigate your life success:

1. Guide
2. Goal
3. Gear

GUIDE

What is a guide, and why would you use one? When you think of a guide, do you think of a person, like the guides who helped me climb Mount Kinabalu, or perhaps a tour guide? When my husband and I travel, we like to find a local guide who can show us all the best things to do, places to see, and places to eat! I love to learn from them and can feel their love for their home and work.

When friends visit you in your hometown, perhaps you have been their guide. People can make great guides in their specific areas of knowledge, interest, and skill. But guides don't have to be people. Experiences, your own and others, can be a helpful guide.

Your past can also stop you from starting if you let it. If an experience and the lessons learned from it are still wrapped in hurt and fear, it may hold you back or even send you in the wrong direction. Do a personal check. Ask yourself, "What lesson can I learn from this experience that will help me grow and move forward?"

Other people's experience can be a great guide and far less costly! You can learn from others through conversations, seminars, a written story, and a checklist, to name a few. Stories are one of my favorite ways to learn from others. They inspire me, give me clarity, and are easy to remember so I can apply them to my life. Their knowledge and wisdom become my guide.

Sometimes you become your own guide; a guide can be internal or external. Internal guides include your values, hopes, dreams, character, and a sense of purpose. How do you choose the direction that is best for you? The answer is to use your internal guides. They become your inner compass. Setting your direction using your internal guides creates alignment, meaning, and joy in your life.

Your internal guide can also direct you to which guides to follow and where not to go. Is what you are proposing aligned with your core values with who you are and want to become? If your proposed action is out of line with your core values, something will not feel right! Your gut, your conscience, that niggly small voice will seek your attention to help you find your best course of action.

But why a guide? What are the benefits of an excellent guide? There is not enough time in life to make all the mistakes yourself and learn from them. A guide does many things. It can provide perspective, prevent you from experiencing setbacks, and save you time and money. A guide can add value and effectiveness to your success growth process and even multiply your success. It can help you choose the best direction for you to achieve success and offer companionship as you start, which enables you to get started well!

How do you pick a guide? Pick a guide who can take you from where you are to where you will go next in an area, subject, or skill that you seek to develop. You may have several guides throughout your journey. This book is a guide to help you start well and build a foundation so you can keep going all the way to your success.

However, not all guides are created equal. Good guiding requires a good relationship between you and your guide. For the best results, choose a guide you can relate to well and whose values align with yours. Trust your gut and your still small voice. If you feel uneasy, that may not be the right guide for you. I look for a guide who has the expertise and skills I need, whose values are in line with mine, and who cannot only teach me a skill but be a role model for me on how to live it.

EXERCISE

Who can help guide you to achieve your goals and dreams?

_____

_____

_____

_____

GOAL

Before you set the course, you need to know two things: where you are and where you want to go. I remember watching the old Westerns. The phrase that sticks in my mind from those movies was "Go west, young man!" I don't know about you, but I'm neither young nor a man, yet that phrase still helps me. My goal and your goal may be a direction rather than a specific place or achievement. Your goal may even be to go nowhere in particular, to wander and explore. "Not all who wander are lost," says J. R. R. Tolkien. Wandering in wonder and exploring can be helpful and powerful goals. Sometimes you are exploring options, discovering who you are and what you can do. So, there is no specific destination.

There is still truth in the idea that when you know where you are going, it is easier to start well. And by starting well, chances are you will finish well. It works particularly well when there is a clear path, and your goal is a specific location to be achieved within a certain timeframe. Such goals are often termed SMART goals. Setting these types of goals can be very helpful in the right context, but they are not the only goals, and for some, goals can be limiting while navigating toward their success. And what about when there is no clear path? What if you are not yet sure what you are looking for? Can you still start well and navigate to reach your goal? Absolutely!

I have run many workshops with people from all walks of life. Many of my clients did not want to set a goal. They had set goals in the past and failed to achieve them. Goals for them meant failure, rejection, and personal worthlessness. I want you to set goals that build you up and move you forward, not tear you down or fill you with fear. This requires a different type of thinking about goals and your relationship with them.

Experience has taught that when people focus on a specific achievement as the goal, they can become stuck, lost, or disappointed when they finally reach their goal. They wonder, *What now? What next?* They haven't thought of the goal as part of their bigger journey. This experience and thinking are known as destination disease. Don't catch it. Destination disease is contagious and debilitating. It can leave you disappointed in yourself or life and stop you from trying to move forward. I used to suffer from destination disease big time. Everything was about my goal and achieving it. I felt dreadful and beat myself up if I didn't reach my goal in the time I wanted. Later, I came to realize that many of the goals I had set for myself were unrealistic. I felt defeated and unworthy because I didn't achieve the unachievable! Now I assess my goals. I make sure they are achievable and give myself the time and resources needed to make them happen. Mostly that works. Sometimes, though, I am overly optimistic and need to reset without judgment and try again.

My ability to navigate my success increased when I learned to work from my purpose down—PURPOSE, VISION, GOAL. This way of thinking works equally well with specific goals, directions, or even when exploring or wandering.

- PURPOSE is the whole life perspective—expressing who I am, why I'm here, and the life I'm seeking to create.

- VISION is what living my purpose looks like for the specific season of my life. If you have a family and young child, your best life in that season will look different than when you were single or when the children have grown and left home.

- GOAL is growing into the person who can live out your vision. "Success is not to be pursued; it is to be attracted by the person you become," says motivational speaker Jim Rohn.

My mentor explained it this way: "Make growth your goal." The gap between where you are and where you want to be is a growth gap. I have discovered by making growth my goal and choosing my direction, with a bit of side wandering and exploring, I am achieving levels of success I had only dreamed of reaching. My process is to make every day a success in the direction of my purpose! I have found this an effective, sustainable, and joyful process to achieve my goals.

EXERCISE

1. My purpose in life is…

_____

_____

_____

_____

2. Living my best life in this season looks like…

_____

_____

_____

_____

3. A goal to help me grow is…

_____

_____

_____

_____

GEAR

To get the job done, you need the right gear, the right resources. You need to be equipped for your success. Gear is not just a tool to navigate or do the work. Gear is not only a warm coat and good boots. Gear includes your mindset and knowledge.

The essential tools you need to navigate are a map and a compass. I touched on these above in the guide section.

The map connects you with your environment. A map opens different ideas and opportunities you did not know existed before. When you want to go somewhere already on a map, it's relatively easy. You can follow the map to wander, explore, or go where you want to go. But if you want to go where "no one has gone before"—whether that new experience is your changing life, a changing world, or something new you want to achieve, you need to create your own map.

When you create your own map, you need to clearly understand what your success looks like. You will need to see your picture of success in your mind's eye before you can arrive. As Reif Larsen shares in the opening quote of this chapter, "A map does not just chart, it unlocks and formulates meaning; it forms bridges between here and there, between disparate ideas that we did not know were previously connected."

Your life is a hands-on navigational experience. Whether following a map or creating one, you will need to respond continually to your changing environment. You will constantly need to make course corrections along the way. Your compass helps you set and hold a direction to stay your course, even when you may temporarily have to change your heading to navigate an obstacle or detour. Your compass uses a standard in which you can see the direction you need to go. Your internal compass is what you stand for, your values, who you are, your talents and passions, and your mindset. They provide the direction to reach where you want to go! It is not set and forget! You will need to actively and intentionally direct your travel, checking and rechecking your direction using your compass.

People talk of being dressed for success. On top of Mount Kinabalu, that meant a warm jacket and winter woolens, even though we were in the tropics. What does being dressed for success mean to you? What does that mean for the fullness of your life's success, not just for work? Throughout this book, you have looked at your success journey. Are you dressed to go the distance, to sustain your journey comfortably? Do you have the flexibility to be ready for the different experiences you will meet? I have seen too many looking great when they start, but like dancers at the party whose shoes do not fit, they soon stop and sit down because their feet hurt, and they cannot keep going. My mental symbol for the gear I need for my success is a pair of hiking boots—comfortable, able to go the distance. But I also pack my dancing shoes!

When you don't have the right gear, it can be hard or even impossible to stay on course. Pause and think about the gear you need to start, keep going, and finish well. What do you need to stop and get now? What can you pick up along the way? What can you put down?

EXERCISE

1. What gear do you need to start?

   _____

   _____

   _____

   _____

2. What are you carrying that no longer serves you that you can put down?

   _____

   _____

   _____

   _____

SUMMARY

1. Actively navigate your life or drift at the mercy of the forces around you.
2. Map and compass are your two main navigational tools.

3. Read maps to navigate the unknown.
4. Chart your maps to navigate the unknown.
5. Your map will unlock meaning and build bridges in your life.
6. Your compass provides direction.
7. The three keys to navigation
    a. Guide
    b. Goal
    c. Gear

Chapter 11

Harnessing the Power of Persistence

"I will persist until I succeed."
Og Mandino

In the previous chapter, we discussed setting your direction and staying aligned with who you are and where you want to go. What comes next? Persistence. Persistence is the make-or-break requirement for success.

Persistence means to keep going. You don't give up. Persistence is about developing a determined attitude combined with action. But you can't continuously live in the red zone—burning the midnight oil and having any quality of life. You must fuel your persistence for the long game. Fuel comes in the form of rest, healthy eating, time for yourself, time for fun, and community.

Developing persistence is about developing the mindset and strategies to "stay in the game." In his book *The Infinite Game*, Simon Sinek says, "You can win in a finite game, like soccer, because there is a set time, set people, set place, set rules, and a clear criterion for when the game ends. That is not so in an infinite game. In an infinite game, the aim is to keep playing, to stay in the game."

There will be many moments when you will want to give up along the road to success. However, because you have prepared yourself to start well and have been equipped to finish well, you will say, "I will not give up. I may change direction, but I will not give up. I will persist until I succeed."

PERSISTING UNTIL IT'S DONE

What is the first thing you think of when you think of Australia and sports? What about Australian Olympic gold medals? When I asked friends this question, they told me they imagine Australia as a place of endless summer and beaches, which is not quite the entire story. Australia has mountains and snowfalls.

Most of Australia's Olympic gold medals have indeed been awarded to Summer Games athletes, but since 1996, Australia has won medals in the Winter Olympics, too. The first Australian Winter Olympic gold medal is a great story of persistence.

It was the 2002 Winter Olympic Games in Salt Lake City, Utah. Steven Bradbury, an Australian short-track speed skater, was skating in his fourth Olympic Games. He was a member of the bronze medal team in 1994, winning Australia's first Winter Games medal!

In 2002, the disqualification of another competitor secured Bradbury's place in the semi-finals. Mindful that he lacked the faster pace of his rivals, Steven chose a strategy to sit at the back of the field and wait for an opportunity. His plan worked to perfection. Opportunity arrived when two of his competitors fell, and another was disqualified. Steven advanced to the finals.

Entering the final race, he chose the same strategy. With only two laps to go, Bradbury was behind the other four competitors. Then it happened! Opportunity showed up again. The other competitors were sliding across the ice—arms, legs, skates, bodies everywhere. Amid this chaos, Bradbury skated past everyone to win Australia's first-ever Winter Olympic Gold. Bradbury became known as the "last man standing" and hailed for winning the unlikeliest gold medal ever. What they called him didn't matter to Bradbury, who stood on the Olympic podium as the Australian national anthem played while he received his gold medal.

Bradbury won not because of luck but because he persisted. His entire career had been one of persistence. He persisted in training despite training for a winter game in a country that had never won any winter Olympic event. He persisted in training to develop the skills needed to qualify for his first Olympic team. Bradbury persisted in returning through four Winter Olympic Games. He persisted through the semi and quarter-finals, taking the opportunities presented. He skated his plan. Then he won, and Australia went wild!

Bradbury's persistence opened the door, and others could see it. His success inspired others. Just days later, Alisa Camplin, drawing inspiration from Bradbury's achievement, somersaulted and landed Australia's first freestyle skiing gold medal. Persistence is contagious. When we see others' hard work pay off, we can dig in and work hard for our hopes and dreams.

I like to call this contagious effect of persistence the "inspiration of perspiration". You may have set out to achieve your own goals and dreams, not inspire others. It doesn't matter. When you persist, you will inspire others. You will become a role model. People will say, "If they can do it, then I can, too." As you persist, who will you inspire? Maybe your son or daughter. Maybe your colleague or friends. Maybe even your critic. As author and comedian Bradley Trevor Greive says in *The Meaning of Life*, "That, my friend, is how you change the world!"

EXERCISE

Where in your life could you benefit from greater persistence?

_____

_____

_____

GOING THE DISTANCE

Bradbury persisted. He went the distance, and so can you. Knowing why, as well as how, will help. During my flight training, my flying instructor explained to me why we did what we did and how. He explained how one control—the throttle—controlled both the power and speed. He explained we use different levels of throttle in different situations.

Taxiing required the pilot to maintain control around other aircraft, with low speed and low throttle. Once on the runway, things changed. When I heard "Clear for takeoff," it signaled time for full throttle. You don't stay at full throttle in flight. If you stayed at full throttle, it would shorten how far you could go. I learned that to sustain our flight, we needed to throttle back and conserve our fuel so we could fly further and for longer.

I have heard some business strategists recommending "full throttle, full speed ahead" to achieve success. Hustle, they say. No, I say. For your sake, your family's sake, your team's sake–NO! Continual hustle is like flying full throttle. It breaks down your power to persist and creates burnout, relationship problems, mental and physical illness, and toxic cultures.

Flying and life experiences teach that a life worth living—a persistent life—needs a different pace, at different times, for different purposes. There will be takeoff and climbing that require full throttle. Then there will be more relaxed, straight-and-level flight times that are low to mid throttle. These low throttle times enable you to travel longer and fly further. There are also times to throttle back, slow down, take time out, refresh, refuel, and renew for the next step in your adventure.

EXERCISE

1. Where do you operate on full throttle?

_____

_____

_____

2. Where do you need to throttle back? How? When?

_____

_____

_____

3. Where do you need to build in rest and refresh opportunities? How? When?

_____

_____

_____

PERSISTING AT LEARNING

To be persistent in life, become persistent in learning. Become a lifelong learner. The internet has opened the door to a new world of learning. You can connect with and learn from someone anywhere in the world. Books are now readily available in hard copy, eBooks, and audiobooks for minimal cost. Learning today goes beyond the classroom and the free resources at the library.

Millions of people take online courses and join special interest communities where knowledge is shared. Whether you want to learn organic farming techniques, business strategies, knitting patterns, or leadership skills, there is an expert you can have immediate access to.

There are three points to consider when you become a lifelong learner:

1. Talent alone is not enough.
   Talent, like everything else in life, requires development. Do you know someone talented but who just gets by? Often people think talent is enough. It's not. Talent alone will take you only so far. You need to put in the effort to master your talent if you want success.

2. We are human beings.
   People who embrace lifelong learning understand that they don't arrive at a finish line. Instead, they see life and learning as an ongoing process of "being." Learning for these people is personal, not just about competence to complete a task. Your lifelong learning will grow out of who you are and what inspires you.

3. What matters?
   If you want life to be more than just a series of days just surviving, develop a habit of lifelong learning. It will support you to live with passion and meaning, following what matters to you, rather than being trapped in the same old same old rut.

EXERCISE

1. What talents could you further develop?

_____

_____

_____

_____

2. What action will you take to develop your talents in line with what matters to you? When?

_____

_____

_____

LEARNING TO SOLVE PUZZLES TOGETHER

Life is not always simple. To persist past the challenges, you will need to become adept at learning to solve the puzzles life throws at you.

I have found some of my best life lessons come from the most ordinary and unexpected moments of life. Have you ever done a giant jigsaw puzzle? Have you tried it without the picture on the lid?

Some of my fondest family memories growing up come from doing jigsaws together. My mum would get out a 1000+ piece jigsaw puzzle. We would all work together putting in a piece or two, go off and do something else, then come back and do some more until we finished it. From doing jigsaws with my mother, I learned the power of persistence—a life lesson that continues to serve me well today.

Now, on holidays, a jigsaw puzzle still comes out. Between meals, beach walks, board games, reading, and other activities, my husband, children, grandchildren, and I all work together to complete the picture—building relationships and developing life skills piece by piece, just like mum and I used to do.

One day, I suddenly thought, *Doing a complex jigsaw puzzle without having a picture on the lid is how many people live their lives.* Is this you? Do you have a picture of what success looks like for you? For your life? The picture of your desired life and future you hold in your mind will drive your persistence and guide you to your success.

Here are five simple lessons from my mum and jigsaw puzzles—five steps that will drive your persistence and success.

FIVE LESSONS FROM A JIGSAW

5 Steps for a Successful Life

1. Choose your puzzle.
2. Set your boundaries.
3. Know your resources.
4. Plan and connect.
5. Dig into the details to repeat and complete.

Step 1

Choose Your Puzzle

In jigsaw puzzle terms, this includes choosing which puzzle you will do. It involves checking the picture on the box and the size. Is it the right jigsaw puzzle for you? Do you have space for it? Can you finish it in the time you have available?

In life terms, this is about becoming more aware—knowing where you are and what is available to you. It's about connecting with your environment and recognizing opportunities and challenges. If your environment does not support your learning and growth, nor sustain your life, choose a new environment.

EXERCISE

What opportunities are available? Where can you find the opportunities you seek?

_____

_____

_____

_____

Step 2

Set Your Boundaries

In jigsaw puzzle terms, this is the edge or the puzzle's frame. Doing the edge first sets you up for success as you progress. Boundaries hold everything together and allow you to get started. They anchor your growth and help you connect individual choices to the bigger picture.

In life terms, boundaries are equally important and perform similar functions. Your boundaries should keep you healthy and include what you will and won't allow into your life. Your boundaries will also facilitate your learning and decision-making.

Setting boundaries can be tricky. Like the jigsaw puzzle, the boundaries you first set may help you get started and make significant progress. Still, your boundaries may require some strengthening, clarification, and change as they are tested. Don't be scared to change and improve your boundaries as you progress.

EXERCISE

What is a boundary you can set to improve your life?

_____

_____

_____

_____

Step 3

Know Your Resources

In jigsaw puzzle terms, you do this by sorting the pieces, grouping like colors and patterns, and setting yourself up to piece them together. Doing a jigsaw is more than solving a puzzle. It is also about appreciating what you have, being happy, feeling togetherness, and experiencing the fun and sense of excitement with what you are creating!

In life terms, this is reflecting and creating alignment between the different pieces of your life and asking what I call the "color questions" of life. Color questions help you live life in full color, not just black, white, or shades of gray. Color questions include feeling and intuition questions. They build your emotional intelligence and assist you in discovering what you want and why. Finding answers to these questions allows you to create a positive and inspiring yet realistic picture of what success looks like for you.

Color questions include: *What puts energy into your emotional tank? What drains it? What makes you laugh? What makes you cry? What are you really feeling now?* Research shows when you become more emotionally aware, you experience greater joy. You will never create a life that feels worthwhile, nor will you appreciate your success without the ability to feel and understand your emotions. Being able to feel and appreciate your success is your ability to add color to your life.

EXERCISE

Where do you want more color in your life?

_____

_____

_____

Step 4

Plan and Connect

In jigsaw puzzle terms, once you have sorted and grouped your pieces, you decide what you do first and then next. You choose based on what connects within the puzzle. As you link sections of pattern and color together, a more detailed framework emerges.

In life terms, this step starts with creating your plan to get started. Once you have a plan to achieve your dreams, priorities, and actions, you choose where to start and what to do next. You identify the skills needed to learn the qualities and fitness you want to develop and the schedule of activities required. Your plan is outcome-focused, but you must balance your schedules to achieve your results within the time and boundaries you have set.

Part of building your plan is connecting with people—the who, what, when, why, and how. Puzzles are a team activity, and so is life. When you work as a team, you share the satisfaction of working towards a common goal and celebrating your result, even preparing to work together on your next adventure.

Who can assist you achieve your success? Here are some questions to consider to help you find your team.

- Who encourages you?
- Who brings out the best in you?
- Who fills you with energy because they are such a joy to be around?
- Who is good at what you want to achieve? How can you learn from them?
- What mentors do you need?
- Who reminds you to get care for yourself so you can persist until you succeed?
- Who works for your best, not what is best for them?
- Who has complementary skills and gifts for you?

EXERCISE

1. Name three people who would support you to persist and succeed if they joined your team.

_____

_____

_____

_____

2. Who can you support?

_____

_____

_____

_____

Step 5

Dig into the Details to Repeat and Complete

With a large puzzle, the simple parts are done first, leaving you with all the difficult, boring bits. Like an immense sky of all the same blue! The advantage is, with all the other pieces in place, you have space—physically and mentally—to focus on the subtle details needed to complete the puzzle. Step five repeats step three and four but at a higher level of detail. Be warned; step five can be the most time-consuming, frustrating, yet critical step for the effective completion of your project.

In life, details matter immensely. Attention to details may mean the difference between a bridge standing or collapsing, the space shuttle returning safely to Earth or crashing, or your meal being a pleasure to eat or a charred sacrifice. Step five is not a unique skill set. It is just a deeper, more detailed level of observation and action. It is the difference between what you see with the first microscope you used in your school science class versus an electron microscope.

LEARNING TO FAIL

The hardest and most traumatic lesson I learned when flying was how to "fail" while in the air and recover. In flying, it means stalling the plane engine at altitude and allowing the plane to begin falling from the sky. Scary and stomach-turning. This lesson is started early in training, with the instructor leading the way.

Why would you want to stop the engine mid-flight, you may ask? Stalling is training in the name of safety and ultimate success. Your rehearsed engine failure is to prepare you to deal with the risk of flying. You learn how to go through "failure" to survive and thrive.

The "failure" training always took place in a designated training area, an airspace with specific geographic and height boundaries that made it safe for the pilots. And for the people who lived, worked, or traveled below, there was time and space to recover from "failure".

I loved learning to fly, but I didn't love these lessons. I still remember the first time the instructor stalled the aircraft. There was my fear factor! Then there was the G-factor, the gravity force that came into play, making me feel I had left my stomach a thousand feet above me. However, I persisted. I learned to overcome my fear. I learned to "fail" and what to do to recover. As I learned, my confidence grew.

I'm sure you have experienced that life does not always go as expected. Perhaps the most important lesson is to learn how and when to get up again when things don't go well or when you fail. Do you have a safe environment in which to fail and recover? Do you have someone who mentors you to move through failure to thrive?

A safe environment is necessary to learn how to fail well and fail forward. If you are a manager, a parent, or a leader, are you creating such an environment for your team, family, or business? Learning to fail is a necessary skill that underlies persistence.

The knowledge that you can fall down, learn, get up, and go again fuels persistence. Persistence builds your competence. Growing competence builds your confidence.

EXERCISE

1. Where has a fear of failure held you back?

_____

_____

_____

_____

2. Who can mentor you to face your fear and push through failure?

_____

_____

_____

_____

SUMMARY

1. Persistence is critical to your success.
2. Play to stay in the game.
3. Nourish yourself for the strength to persist.
4. Persistence creates opportunities, and you will inspire others.
5. Persist in learning; be a lifelong learner.
6. Learn to persist through failure.
7. Develop an environment, at home and at work, where it is safe to fail.
8. Manage the pace of your life.
9. 5 Steps for Success from jigsaws and my mum:
    a. Choose your puzzle
    b. Set your boundaries
    c. Know your resources
    d. Plan and connect
    e. Dig into details

Chapter 12

Releasing Your Power Through Habits

"Motivation is what gets you started. Habit is what keeps you going."
Jim Rohn

Motivation wanes over time. That is why your habits matter. In the previous chapter, you looked at persistence. Habits add consistency to persistence. Using the power of habits in your life is the best way to ensure you can persist and sustain your success.

Our habits are the patterns in our behavior and thinking. Some behaviors we have settled into and therefore fail to be aware of them. We don't question the things we do. To improve our habits, we must first become aware of them, then ask ourselves if they serve us.

Habits are often thought of as automatic responses—no thinking required. I've got good news. Many habits over time become automatic, and they need to be in order to support your journey. But higher level, transformational habits—also called meta-habits—are deliberate and more conscious, built by your intentional choice. You choose a new habit based on what is important to you, what you value, and what you seek to create.

Research has shown that behind each habitual action lies habitual thinking. Your thinking habits also become automatic unless you challenge and change your thinking patterns. To change your behavior habits, you will need to change your thinking habits.

Habits can be internal or external focused. Internal habits include your thinking, emotional reactions, and self-talk. Internal habits are identity-based. External habits include how you interact with your environment. External habits are outcomes-based. Transformational habit change happens from the internal to the external.

One thing that all researchers and writers on habits agree on is that habits are powerful. Your habits create you and create your life—for better, for worse. If you do not control your habits, your habits will control you. Success is gained by making small, positive, healthy habit choices a daily part of your everyday living. These consistent slight changes or micro-habits compound over time, creating huge results.

The power of habits is not a new idea. The 17th Century poet, John Dryden, said, "We first make our habits, then our habits make us." Aristotle, philosopher and student of Plato, is credited with saying, "We are what we repeatedly do. Excellence is not an act, but a habit."

Assessing your habits as healthy or helpful, rather than good or bad, right or wrong, can help you choose the best action to take. Healthy and helpful habits support your success by building a better you. Unhealthy and unhelpful take you away from your success or create barriers to it. Evaluate your internal habits according to whether they promote health and help you grow to a better, stronger version of yourself. Evaluate your external habits to determine whether they are helpful or unhelpful, taking you towards what you seek to create or away from it. To release your power through habits, you will need to exchange your unhealthy habits for healthier ones and your unhelpful habits for more helpful ones.

Habits change by choice, deliberate action, and changing contexts. Your world is changing. As a result, your habits change. Those changing habits then further change in our world. So, what can you and I do to move forward? How can we build positive habits that will serve us well? When things change in your life, you will need to pause and ask yourself, "Do my current habits still serve me well?" and "What current habits do I need to challenge and change to succeed in my changing world?" Some habits will need to change. Some won't.

Your success journey and habit development need to cover the full breadth of what is important in your life, including physical and mental health habits and creating positive relationships.

CREATING THE NEW YOU

In his book *Atomic Habits*, James Clear sums up the importance of habits: "Ultimately your habits matter because they help you become the type of person you wish to be. They are the channel through which you develop your deepest beliefs about yourself. Literally, you become your habits." James Clear shows that habits are also important because success is not a goal.

Success is "a system to improve and an endless process to refine." Your collection of daily habits is your system. You will rise, or you will fall, to the level of your systems. He adds, "Habits are the compound interest of self-improvement… They seem to make little difference on any day, and yet the impact they deliver over the month and years can be enormous. You get what you repeat." Do you want more success, faster? The compounding impact of your habits is the way to achieve your success.

I want to live long enough to see my grandkids become adults and meet my great-grandchildren. I want to tell them I love them. This vision inspired me to reflect on and change my habits. I thought back to meeting my great, great aunt Clara, who was 100 years old. My children had the privilege of meeting their 97-year-old great grandfather in England. I thought about my grandmother and my husband's mother and their joy when they spent time with their grandkids and great-grandkids.

That's when I decided that's what I want! I want to be a healthy, happy, active 90-plus, enjoying my grandkids and dancing at their weddings. I want to speak love and hope into their lives. And I want to role-model caring and living every day of my life, whatever my age. So now, I get to choose the habits that help me become that person.

What about you? What is so important it would be worth changing your habits to achieve it?

EXERCISE

What is so important you will change your habits to achieve it?

_____

_____

HEALTHY HABITS KEEP YOU GOING

You have probably heard, "You are what you eat," and "Use it or lose it." Have you ever eaten a meal and felt like taking a nap afterwards? Have you ever felt like not exercising but did it anyway? Did you feel energized after exercising and glad you made the effort? I can say yes to all of the above. What about you?

For years, I experienced low energy after eating starchy or sweet foods. By the end of the meal, I could feel my energy draining away. As I became more health-conscious and self-aware, I started eating more foods that energized me. When I made this change, I felt better, was happier, slept better, enjoyed exercise more, and carried less weight. People even commented I looked better. Bonus! The change did not happen with the first meal. Instead, it happened over a series of healthy choices.

I learned healthy habits increased my energy. Unhealthy habits weighed me down in more ways than one. I followed a simple four-step program to keep my energy high. I use these same steps to help choose my healthy, helpful habits.

1. Good in
2. Bad out
3. Exercise (use) what you have
4. Create a positive environment

Leadership coach, John Maxwell, says, "You will never change your life until you change something you do daily." Our habits become not a task to achieve but a lifestyle to live daily. Micro-habits are habits small enough and easy enough to do every day. For example, the lifestyle commitment, or macro-habit, of healthy hydration (drinking more water) can be supported by drinking a glass of water first thing in the morning, a micro-habit.

Micro-habits are easiest to establish when there is a trigger—a set time, place, or event to start the action—and a reward that makes you want to keep repeating the habit. For example, one of my triggers is making a cup of tea. Whenever I make a cup of tea, I do a bench push-up or a squat. Sometimes I do ten, but the simple action I chose to do is one bench push-up! When done, my reward is to enjoy my cup of tea and feel good about myself. You can create your own micro-habit, trigger, and reward that supports your healthy goal.

As Jim Rohn said in the opening quote of this chapter, healthy habits will keep you going.

EXERCISE

1. Rate yourself on a scale from 1 (low) to 10 (high) on each of the macro health habits.

    ☐ Healthy weight management _____
    ☐ Healthy eating and hydration _____
    ☐ Healthy motion _____
    ☐ Healthy sleep _____
    ☐ Healthy mind _____
    ☐ Healthy surroundings _____

ACTION

1. Pick one habit you would like to improve.

    _____
    _____
    _____
    _____

2. Identify one micro-habit that will support you in achieving your goal.

    _____
    _____
    _____
    _____

3. Pick an easy trigger to do it.

_____

_____

_____

_____

4. Start today!

_____

_____

_____

_____

HABITS OF BUILDING STRONG RELATIONSHIPS

One of my most beautiful memories of my husband and my time at college came from a seminar on building strong marriages. You may have heard the expression "the straw that broke the camel's back." That seminar helped my husband and me recognize straws that could break the camel's back in our relationship—the little negative micro-habits of thought and action that allow aggravation and disappointment to build up. It showed us that we need to always be prepared to have tough conversations whenever required and address the issue before it becomes "the straw" that will break the back of our marriage.

College principal Dr. Arthur Cundall, and his wife, Joyce, who had been married for over forty years, led the seminar. They spoke of the power of habits to keep your marriage strong and fresh. Dr. Cundall asked us to remember how we felt when we first started dating. He asked us to remember the little things we said and did in the beginning to show our love and appreciation for each other. He then asked us if we were still giving and receiving those small expressions of affection every day?

The Cundalls went on to share a story about when their relationship was at a crossroads—a story about toothpaste. When they first married, Dr. Cundall explained he used to set out their toothbrushes and put toothpaste on both his and Joyce's toothbrush to show Joyce how much he cared for her. The problem came when he stopped.

The message received by Joyce was not the one Dr. Cundall intended—"It is time for you to start putting your own toothpaste on your toothbrush now." The message communicated was, "I don't care for you anymore. I don't love you anymore."

Something as simple and outwardly insignificant as not putting toothpaste on a toothbrush almost cost them their marriage. Dr. Cundall said, "When we stopped and faced what was happening, we both knew we had to recreate little daily habits that affirmed each other and fed our relationship. We would continue to hurt if we didn't, and our marriage would fail."

Dr. Cundall concluded, "It's not that hard to turn a hurting marriage around. Just do the little things that built the strong relationship in the first place and keep doing them. Build trust by keeping your word and doing the little caring habits to strengthen your relationship."

Now, it is my husband and me who have been married for over forty years. I wish I could tell you hearing that one story meant all our issues were sorted forever, but that wouldn't be true. What is true, though, is the toothpaste story has helped us have the hard conversations. We recognized where our habits needed to be re-examined and changed. We create daily habits that feed our relationship. One habit we do is to tell each other "I love you" every day.

Strong relationships are built by consistent, positive habits of open, non-judgmental communication, listening, and reflection. Even when you don't see the impact immediately, remember the compound effect and keep doing the healthy, helpful building habits. Also, remember what got you this far may not take you where you want to go. Some habits that served you well in the past may need to be changed to build the future you desire. Continue to ask yourself if the habit is healthy or helpful. If not, change it.

MAKING TIME YOUR ALLY

The compounding effect of habits works negatively and positively. When productivity, knowledge, and healthy relationships compound, there is a positive effect. There is a negative effect when stress, negative thoughts, and anger compound. With healthy and helpful habits, time becomes your ally. With unhealthy and unhelpful habits, you make time for the enemy.

EXERCISE

1. Where are you experiencing positive compounding effects of your habits? What is one thing you can do to improve this effect?

   _____

   _____

   _____

   _____

2. Where are you experiencing negative compounding effects of your habits? What is one thing you can do to replace a negative habit with a positive one?

   _____

   _____

   _____

   _____

IMPROVING YOUR HABITS

Developing good habits sounds easy, but is it? How do you choose the best habits for you, your situation, and the results you want to achieve?

You may already know which habits would improve your life, but you are not doing them. Why not? Have you tried in the past and failed? Are you fearful of failing again or doubting whether anything can work for you?

So how do you choose the best habits and stick with them? You start with you and your identity. Your identity is your repeated beingness. Identity is about what you believe. It is not set; you can change your identity. At the beginning of this chapter, we talked about internal and external habits. The best way to change your habits is from the inside out. Start with who you wish to become and what you believe rather than what you seek to have. When your WHY and identity are linked, your success is well on its way! This direction of change is important to achieve lasting results. It often helps to find a mentor when designing your healthy habits.

When you know who you want to be and your powerful WHY, you can move your focus from dreaming about what you want to achieve to learning how to get it. If you make the change by focusing on the external first, that will likely lead to you giving up or failing. For example, you may want the energy to play with your kids or grandkids, or maybe you want to be recognized as the top performer at your job and receive a promotion. Whatever you choose, imagine yourself as the person who can live your dreams and act in a way that creates how you think of yourself—your new identity.

FROM WHY TO WHAT AND HOW

After WHY comes WHAT.

This WHAT is about creating further clarity and direction. Then your micro-habits are your HOW. Your small, daily actions create the change, but it takes time to see and feel the difference. Your strong WHY gives you power and buys you the passion-driven time you need to succeed. Therefore, your WHY is so important!

An effective habit method looks like:

- WHY – your identity
- WHAT – the outcome
- HOW – your micro-habit, the daily repeated action that compounds to achieve your WHAT
- WHEN – your trigger or calendar event that makes the action easy to do
- WITH WHOM – your mentor, your role model, your support person or team

EXERCISE

1. What is the top priority habit you want to improve?

_____

_____

2. Write out statements that support you in building your new habit? (E.g. I am a healthy person. I am a non-smoker. I am generous and caring.)

   _____
   _____
   _____
   _____

3. What daily action will you take? Starting when?

   _____
   _____
   _____

4. When will you do it? What is your trigger event?

   _____
   _____
   _____

5. Who can support you in making this change?

   _____
   _____
   _____

SUCCESS THROUGH HABIT

Different habits support different levels of performance. Athletics is a great example of this. The habits of an Olympic runner differ from the person who wants to run twice a week to keep fit. Both people can be a success in their pursuit yet have different habits to achieve that success.

You choose habits that create your high-performance life based on areas of priority for your life. According to Brendon Burchard in his book *High Performance Habits*, a high performer is "someone who creates ever-increasing levels of both well-being and external success over the long term." Over the long term is key. Top performers are consistent. They are not "peak performers" who peak and then burn out. Because well-being is built into their habits, what they achieve is sustainable.

Brendon Burchard says, "High performance happens because of what you think and do in order to excel and serve at higher levels." High-performance habits predict not just performance but also happiness. High performance, well-being, happiness, and service are a collection of outcomes worth putting some effort behind. High performers build successful lives by making each day a success.

What is fascinating about the research into these high-performance habits is that an improvement in one area spills over and improves the other areas, too.

Success through habit comes back to the same essential ingredients you saw in building healthy habits. Thoughtful, intentional choice supported by daily actions becomes part of who you are, and therefore, how you act. Can you be a high performer? Yes, you can. You can be happier. You can experience higher performance levels, better relationships, and a better life by building higher performance habits in your life.

SUMMARY

1. Habits are repeated action or ways of thinking.
2. Habits can be automatic or intentional.
3. Habits are powerful.
4. Your habits create your identity.
5. You become your habits.
6. Control your habits, or your habits control you.
7. Healthy habits increase your energy.
8. Triggers and rewards can help embed positive new habits.
9. Good habits make time your ally.
10. High-performance habits lead to increased performance and happiness.

Chapter 13
Being Resilient

"The brook would lose its song if you removed the rocks."
Fred Beck

Let's take a moment to reflect on how far you have come. You have learned how to prepare for your journey and set yourself up for success. You have stepped out on your adventure and now understand how to connect to the world around you, setting your direction that aligns with your identity and life. You're building strength. You are moving forward, step by step, with persistence and developing habits that support you in times of challenge. You build resilience when you put your positive mindset, knowledge, and skills together. Everyone goes off track at some point as they navigate success. Resilience allows you to get back on track!

Resilience historically means to leap back. It is the capacity to recover quickly from your difficulties—to be stretched and spring back into shape. Have you noticed that some people are fantastic at that, while others of us not so much? In personal growth terms, resilience means the ability to regain a sense of happiness and purpose after something difficult or bad has happened. The ability to bounce back and be happy again is resilience that can be learned and strengthened.

Bounce back, recover from difficulties, get back on track, and be happy again. Yes, you can experience all these. You can be resilient.

THE CRY OF THE 21ST CENTURY

Developing resilience is not new, but the call for increased resilience is everywhere. "We need to build resilience in our people" is a cry heard everywhere. There are many models, resources, and training provided to teach how to increase resilience. They all have one common idea: by strengthening the components of resilience, we become more resilient.

WHAT IS RESILIENCE, AND WHY DOES IT MATTER?

What is resilience, and why does it matter?

"When things go wrong, resilience is what helps you cope and get through hard times. Sometimes it makes you even stronger than you were before," from the website Kids Helpline.

Resilience matters because it helps you get through and bounce back, often even stronger than before. It strengthens you in a way that you can hold your head up, which can be a challenge when you are hurting.

Your resilience is not fixed. It is not something you were lucky enough to be born with it. Resilience is something you choose to develop and grow.

WHAT DEVELOPS RESILIENCE?

Here are some simple pointers from Kids Helpline on what builds resilience and how you, I, and those we care for can develop it.

Some things that develop resilience:

- Having a positive attitude
- Finding good friends
- Feeling good about yourself
- Feeling you belong
- Helping others or "giving back" (a big one!)
- Learning how to solve problems and overcome challenges
- Good communication skills
- Connecting with surrounding people (very important!)

If you don't have these, don't worry. You can still develop these things and become resilient. Focus on what you have and what you can control. Resilience is still there for you!

I have found that stories of resilience can inspire resilience. The following story has inspired me to keep building resilience in my life. I hope it also encourages you to find hope, act, and build resilience in your life.

If the story triggers negative responses in you, be courageous and get the help you need.

DEFINING MOMENTS

I first heard the story of Frank, an Army Ranger and Vietnam veteran, when I started working with his lovely wife, Dorothy. Dorothy shared what she and I were doing together with Frank. Our work seemed to resonate with him, and Frank sent me a copy of his stories about his military service in Vietnam and gave me permission to share them with you.

In one of Frank's stories, *Death of Innocence*, Frank describes an incident that occurred while he was on patrol. Hearing what sounded like someone approaching, Frank hid in the brush, and in the dim light, he saw four armed Viet Cong only 20-30 feet away. Frank says, "What happened in the next two minutes defined the next forty-five years of my life."

EXERCISE

1. Is there an event in your life that defines your life?

_____

_____

_____

_____

Frank had it all in his career, but then, "it all" came crashing down. "There really was nothing left to live for," Frank says, but three connections saved his life and planted the seeds of resilience.

1. The Battalion Chaplain. (They are still friends today over fifty years later.)
2. A change of command. The new commander listened, showed him respect, challenged him with a meaningful job, and provided

Frank with the mental and emotional support he needed.
3. A friendly letter from his old girlfriend. Two months after Frank returned to the USA, Dorothy and Frank were married and are still married over fifty years later.

BUILDING RESILIENCE THROUGH FINDING CONNECTION

The hurt from Frank's defining moment was deep, and it is only in the last few years that Frank has written his stories. Frank's story shows that deep hurt need not stop you from becoming resilient. Rather the hurt becomes your pathway to resilience. His story also shows that the resilience journey may not be fast or easy, but it is real and possible no matter what happened or where you started.

In *Hitting Bottom*, Frank starts strong, saying, "If you have post-traumatic stress, you really only have two choices; you live with it, or you die." He continues, "If you decide to live, you have two choices. You can live the rest of your life with post-traumatic stress, or you can decide to get better. If you decide to live with it, then you will live the rest of your life miserable and make everyone you love miserable too. Why would you want to do that? So, in reality, the only viable option is for you to get well."

Again, Frank outlines his two choices: "Attempt to do it on your own or get someone to help you." Then he admonishes himself: "When you were shot, you didn't stop the bleeding and sew yourself up alone, did you? When you had cancer, you didn't cut it out all by yourself, did you? So why the hell would you try to cure yourself of post-traumatic stress? It makes no more sense than shooting yourself. Which is probably what you will wind up doing anyway if you try this on your own."

CHOOSING TO EMBRACE THE RESILIENCE PROCESS

"I did something," said Frank.

Frank sought help. First from his pastor, who wasn't equipped to help him. Stop two was an Army chaplain whose church sponsored a counseling program. The program and the person did not fit— zero connection. The next stop to seek help was the Veteran's Hospital. In the mental health ward, he was assigned a social worker/counselor who Frank describes as "so light in the loafers that he floated around the room. Not exactly a strong rapport builder with an Airborne Ranger." He notes, "At the end of every session, he would say, 'Well, I think you are now cured. How do you feel?'" Frank adds, "I lasted four sessions before I agreed I was 'cured'."

NOT GIVING UP, NOT GIVING IN

Frank admits nothing seemed to work, but he knew he needed help and needed it quick. "I gave the Veterans Administration (VA) one more go. I drove to the local VA clinic fifteen minutes from my house. When the nurse asked me what I wanted, I told her I needed to see a doctor. She looked at her computer screen and replied, 'The first available appointment to see a doctor is in three months.' That was not the answer I was looking for. After she assured me that she was not joking, I told her, 'I appreciate your interest in National Defense, but I need to see a doctor now. Not in three months, not in three weeks, not in three days, not even in three hours. You have three minutes to get me in to see someone, or I can assure you that once the note attached to my body saying I was turned away at the VA clinic, you and probably every other person in this clinic will wish their mothers had not met their fathers.' I saw Ms. Jackson in under three minutes." Frank says of Ms. Jackson, "Ms. Jackson is a big black lady. I loved her immediately—like talking to my mother, only better."

Two hours later, Frank left with an appointment at the VA hospital where he had been "cured". This time, his appointment was with a "real live" psychiatrist, Dr. G. "Seeing a real psychiatrist in the VA system was a miracle," says Frank.

Frank connected and persisted again, and his resilience strengthened. Frank says after two months, he was tricked by Dr. G. into joining a six-month program from a friend of hers, Dr. H., who specialized in post-traumatic stress. That, says Frank, was his second miracle.

Dr. H. was even better than Dr. G! Frank trusted her immediately. Dr. H. cut to the chase with Frank.

Frank says, "Dr. H. explained that she had a six-month program that would help me tremendously if I put in the time and effort. Dr. H. said that the program was challenging and sometimes very stressful. Many started but didn't finish. However, Dr. H. also said if I saw it through to the end, the results would be worth it. I told Dr. H. that if I started something, I always finished it, and I would accept her challenge. I wanted to get better, and I didn't enjoy taking drugs."

Looking back, Frank now talks of those six months. "Dr. H. was right. It was a tough six months, but I finished the program, and, true to her word, I am better—much, much better. I am not cured. I don't know if a person is ever really cured of post-traumatic stress, but I'm much better. I still take prescription drugs, but not as many."

In thankfulness, Frank dedicated one of his stories to Dr. H. Frank had many opportunities to stop and give up, but he didn't. Today he holds his head up high.

Reflecting on the entire experience, Frank asks, "What was the turning point? What was the one thing that made all the difference?" His conclusion, "I really don't know. There were exercises in Dr. H.'s six-month therapy that really helped. Talking really helped. Support from my wife really helped. But I don't think there is any magic bullet except commitment. But I think the real turning point was reaching rock bottom and deciding I didn't want to die. I told myself I was going to do whatever it took to make myself better. And I did."

Resilience starts with a simple decision to live and keep going!

Thank you, Frank, for deciding you didn't want to die and doing whatever it took. Your commitment and courage are an inspiring role model of resilience.

FROM THE OTHER SIDE – PARTNERS IN THE RESILIENCE JOURNEY

I already had permission to share Frank's story when I wrote the above, but I wanted to check that I hadn't misunderstood or misrepresented anything. Frank and his wife, Dorothy, read the draft together. "Go ahead," came the reply before dinner. The next morning, I received Dorothy's "I've slept on it" email. Her response added greater depth and clarity to understanding the resilience journey and its impact on those we love and care about.

Dorothy wrote, "When you noted that the next few minutes would define his life for the next forty-five years, I think it's important to share that Frank locked his experiences in the war zone—the horror deep within— and never talked about any of it for 40+ years." Dorothy went on to explain, "War is hell on earth. The damage to the soul is real. When Dr. H's program required Frank to begin writing, Frank had to make a personal decision to accept the challenge. He had to go deep inside and bring these buried memories to the surface. For months, he went through horrible nightmares, night sweats, screaming out from his sleep in horror. Yet he remained committed to healing, going through the pain, facing his demons, and ultimately living."

Dorothy added, "It wasn't just Frank who had to take the resilience journey. Frank had the nightmares. I had Frank having the nightmares, and all the rest!"

EXCISING THE WOUND

Stuffing hurt inside for years in hopes that it will affect only you and keep a loved one safe is a common story, but it is a lie. Suppressing the hurt and pain does not serve you, and it does not serve them. The wound becomes infected and can infect your whole life. Find help. Excise your wound. The earlier, the better.

Dorothy also corrected my timing assumption. She wrote, "As I reflect, I realize Frank chose life twice—first in Vietnam as a chaplain cared for him and worked with him, then again, forty-five years later when he went through two cancer surgeries within two years triggered by exposure to Agent Orange. Cancer brought Frank to where he went to the VA and was admitted. After forty-five years, he needed help and insisted he must see a doctor. It was then that God brought in Mrs. Jackson, who genuinely cared, listened with her heart, and took immediate action." Dorothy said, "I believe God always has these people there, if only we will admit we need help and do the work to get better. Frank's story bears testimony to this truth."

IT IS YOUR TIME

It took Frank forty-five years, but you don't have to wait any longer. If you are holding on to something that needs to come out, don't wait—whether it is weeks, months, or a lifetime. Like Frank, choose life. Choose to take your resilience journey today!

EXERCISE

1. Who cares for you?

　

2. What does "choose life" mean to you?

　

3. Where do you need to "do whatever it takes"?

　

4. Where and from whom can you get the help you need?

GROWING RESILIENCE

You don't have to have experienced trauma to develop resilience. Two of my favorite inspirational books are by an Australian author and humourist, Bradley Trevor Greive, known as BTG. They are *The Blue Day Book, A Lesson in Cheering Yourself Up* and *The Meaning of Life*, which I referenced in the previous chapter. BTG's crazy, fun books have been sold over 30 million copies in 115 countries, but he wasn't always a success, and he wasn't always an author. Twenty years after first publishing *The Blue Day Book*, BTG released an illustrated version of the same book, which includes a note from the author, where he tells his story of how he became a writer. It is a classic tale of resilience.

Like Frank, BTG was a soldier, a graduate of Australia's Royal Military College, and a former paratrooper commander. BTG's need for resilience was not PTSD. He got sick, and his life fell apart.

"A tropical lung infection," he says, "led to the sudden demise of my promising military career. Worst of all, I could do nothing about it but weep tears of pain and rage."

Suppose you have lost your career or your dream. In that case, you may identify with BTG when he states, "Then after an especially rotten day, at the end of a very tough week, in the middle of an awful month, during a very difficult year, I hit rock bottom like a concrete pancake. Lonely, ill, and unable to find a steady job or a steady girlfriend, I was stupendously broke."

HITTING ROCK BOTTOM

You don't need nor do you develop resilience on good days. Resilience is demanded and grown when you feel most unable to give it. But the good thing about hitting rock bottom is that it is the bottom. From the bottom, you can push off and up. Hitting bottom can become a new direction, a new beginning.

BTG shares, "I was so frustrated and embarrassed by the miserable direction my life had taken, and yet I only made things worse by running away from my problems."

Resilience doesn't look like much when you hit bottom—like the quote, "Open heart surgery, halfway through, looks more like murder than a life-saving operation." Turning hitting rock bottom from an ending into a new beginning is the gift of resilience. Resilience is like a muscle. Feed and exercise your resilience, and it will grow. Bradley Trevor Greive's story reminded me of the quote from Winston Churchill: "When you're going through hell, don't stop. Keep going." BTG kept going. He fed his resilience.

EXERCISE

In what ways have you hit rock bottom? What could you stop running from?

_____

_____

_____

_____

FEEDING RESILIENCE

Frank and Bradley Trevor Greive came to their resilience journeys via very different trigger experiences. I don't know what you have faced, are facing, or will face. What I do know is you will be given the opportunity to practice and grow resilience at different times in your life—when your experiences will challenge your identity to the core. Your thoughts and emotions will threaten to paralyze, stop, or overwhelm you. But as you navigate through to the other side, you will come out stronger, and your stories will inspire others. Frank and BTG have shown you that moving through hurt, difficulty, and pain is possible and worth it. You are aware. You are forearmed. You are prepped for greater resilience.

Frank and Bradley Trevor Greive completed many of the recommendations to build resilience. Let's take a quick look.

1. Make a connection with friends and family.
2. Give things a go.
3. Face what is real. Be honest, no blaming.

4. Ask for help. No one must face struggles alone. It is courageous to ask for help.
5. Get back in shape. Look after your physical health, which has a big impact on mental and emotional health.
6. Serve others.

EXERCISE

What will you do to feed your resilience and bounce back stronger?

_____
_____
_____
_____

"Don't let what you can't do stop you from doing what you can," are wise words from Coach John Wooden. Your path may have many steps—some you are not yet ready to take. Your journey is your journey. Building connections is part of the resilience journey. If connecting with others is too big of a step, you may find a connection with an animal a fantastic first step. There are assistance dogs and horse-based programs to help rebuild connections and strengthen resilience. Check out programs near you. Start where you are and do what you can. It is a journey, but not a race.

EXERCISE

1. What did you relate to most in Frank and BTG's stories?

_____
_____
_____
_____

2. What action will assist you in building resilience in your life?

_____

_____

_____

CHOOSE LIFE

On December 1, 2017, a Facebook post popped up in my feed. Another veteran had committed suicide. I walked outside. I cried and cried out. I have lost two very dear friends to suicide. Despair is real. Teenage suicide is real. I've seen the impact, and no, the family is NOT better off without you.

After walking back inside, I wrote a poem titled "Choose Life". Resilience is a choice, your choice. Like Frank and BTG, you have the opportunity to choose life and choose your resilience journey. When you face that choice, this poem is for you.

I CHOOSE LIFE

I choose life.
I feed myself
…despite the pain, darkness, and loss.
I choose life.
I feed health
…of body, mind, and spirit.
I choose life.
I feed hope
…of life, purpose, and me.
I choose life.
I feed strength
…to walk, grow, and renew.
I choose life.
I feed connection
…to heal, learn, and trust again.
I choose life.
I feed vision
…of love, family, and friendship.
I choose life.
I feed the light
I choose to live, give, serve – today
I choose life.

SUMMARY

1. Whatever your situation, you can bounce back. You can be resilient.
2. There is always hope.
3. Others have shown you a path through.
4. You can hold your head up again.
5. You can come back stronger than before.
6. Resilience is a choice.
7. Connection builds resilience.
8. Resilience is grown and strengthened by your choices.
9. Hitting "rock bottom" is your opportunity for your new beginning.
10. Do what you can. Take your first step.
11. Choose life.

Chapter 14

Showing the Way

"Climb every mountain, ford every stream, follow every rainbow until you find your dream."
Rogers & Hammerstein, Lyrics from The Sound of Music

If it seems to you that everything worthwhile is an uphill climb, be encouraged. The road to success is a winding road, and it often feels uphill. With this lesson, you are almost at the top of this mountain. Since starting this book, what has changed for you? What is different about how you see yourself, your life, and your future?

Because you have come this far in your journey, you are ready to climb higher and see further. As you continue, what was once a hope a short while ago is becoming a reality. These new hopes, possibilities, dreams, and visions of success replace older ones. Nelson Mandela said, "After climbing a great hill, one finds there are more hills to climb." For you, now is the time to keep going. Your next adventure, your next milestone, your next mountain awaits you.

CLIMBING HIGH

Have you ever climbed a mountain and reached a place where you could stand and survey the amazing view before you? How far could you see? How did you feel? What were your thoughts?

Standing surrounded by snow, looking down over the border wall into Mexico, seeing the route that the first Spanish conquistadors took to enter what is now the USA is one mountaintop experience I will never forget. The road to the top of the mountain was slippery from the recent snow. Even in our four-wheel-drive vehicle, our guide traveled slowly and carefully.

The higher we drove, the further we could see through gaps in the surrounding hills, then over the top of the near hills to the other hills and plains beyond. We parked and continued on foot to the mountain peak. As I stood there in awe, taking in all 360 degrees of the valley below and the mountains surrounding us, I was struck by the view and combined impact of the history. People from countless cultures had stood here for hundreds of years. I felt in that moment I understood for the first time what it meant to "stand on the shoulders of giants." The past gave meaning to this present moment and possibility for the future.

EXERCISE

1. What is your mountaintop experience(s)?

___

___

___

___

2. What made it so special?

___

___

___

___

FINDING YOUR MOUNTAIN

There were and still are many mountains to climb, rivers to ford, and dreams to pursue in my life. Some of my mountains might be a hill to someone else. It doesn't matter what others call it. It is still a mountain to me, and I still need to climb it!

The words of the song "Climb Every Mountain" from *The Sound of Music* have become part of my identity. My mountains are the challenges. The streams to ford are the dangers I face. The standout theme for me of *The Sound of Music* is courage—courage to face life, start anew, and follow through. It has taught me how to have the courage to stand for who I am and what I believe in, and it strengthened my courage to climb higher, see farther, and climb again. The song's words inspire me every day to keep climbing to reach my dreams. I sing the words to myself when I need courage. I sang that song softly to my three-week-old grandson as I held him in my arms during days spent in the special care nursery after a difficult birth. I thought I was alone, but unknown to me, another mom was quietly sitting with her newborn just a few feet away, facing her own child's challenges. I sang it repeatedly. The next morning, the mother who had overheard me came and said, "Thank you. I heard you singing the song from *The Sound of Music* last night. Your singing was beautiful. It really helped. That message made my day."

Supporting a newborn struggling for life is certainly a mountain to climb and a dangerous river that must be crossed. What are your mountains to climb? Are there potentially dangerous rivers you need to cross to reach your dream? What feeds your courage to keep climbing?

EXERCISE

What life challenges are you facing that appear to be mountains?

_____

_____

_____

_____

As I sang, I was just being a grandma, trying to support my grandson and daughter. But, in being me, I connected unknowingly to someone I had never met. Maya Angelou says, "The area where we are the greatest is the area in which we inspire, encourage, and connect with another human being." Your journey may have meant you already connected with and inspired someone. Or it may mean you will.

I don't know where you were physically, emotionally, mentally, or spiritually when you started this book, but what I know is you have come this far.

And you have changed because of what you have learned and practiced each day. You are stronger, better able to navigate life, and have increased confidence and courage. You better understand how starting well will help you finish well.

As we have traveled this journey together, you have faced your darkness and turned on your light within. As it lights your path, your light will also light the paths of others. Because of you, others are choosing to start! Do not be scared or hide. Don't hide your light. Each day, allow yourself to be real, to be seen. Each day, you will influence others. Your vulnerability will give them the courage to start their journey!

In the chapter on resilience, you met the author Bradley Trevor Greive. I was struggling when I first saw the picture of the smiling seal and read the crazy words, "Doing the things that make your whiskers curl with delight (assuming, of course, that you actually have whiskers), you will inspire someone else to go after their dreams. And that, my friend, is how you change the world!"

Over 2000 years ago, it was written, "No one lights a lamp and puts it under a bowl; instead, they put it on the lampstand, where it gives light for everyone in the house. In the same way, your light must shine before people so that they will see the good things you do…" When you shine your light, you show the way for others to follow.

THE TORCH IS PASSED

Prior to the opening of the 2000 Sydney Olympic Games, the Olympic flame was lit in Athens and carried around Australia by Olympic torch relay runners. The runners were old and young, big and small, male and female, from diverse cultures and backgrounds. Some were even in wheelchairs. They carried that flame across the width and breadth of Australia before it reached the Sydney Olympic Stadium, heralding the start of the games. Wherever the torch went, people came out and cheered for the torchbearers. My husband and I joined a small group as the torchbearer appeared on the horizon. Together, we watched as one runner passed the baton to the next, right where we were standing. We cheered and even shed a tear. So powerful was the experience.

Now it is your turn. The torch is in your hands. It is your turn to show the way. Each day, step up and step out—do the next right thing. In doing so, you will live and be the success you desire, where it matters most to you. Be true to who you are and what you stand for. Share your journey. Share your story. Shine your light.

Every new beginning starts with an ending. As this chapter ends, your new journey is just beginning. Start well!

SUMMARY
1. You are greatest when you connect with and inspire others.
2. Let your light shine.
3. Your light will guide others.
4. You have a story that will inspire and empower others.
5. The torch is in your hands.
6. In giving, you will receive.
7. Your journey is just beginning.

Chapter 15
Continuing Your Adventure

"Life is a daring adventure or nothing at all."
Helen Keller

Beware! Now is a dangerous time for you! It is easy to finish a book, put it back on the shelf, and forget it. If you do that, you will stop growing, stop moving forward, and slide back into old habits that do not serve the new you. You have come too far to stop and slide back. You are made of stronger stuff than that!

We have journeyed together through the pages of this book, and you have pushed through the darkness and climbed your mountains. On this journey, you have smiled, laughed, and reflected on deep truths about who you are, the life you live, and the life you want to create.

I challenge you to act. Now. Today while the momentum is strong. Knowledge is an open door, but you still need to walk through it. On its own, knowledge is not power. "Applied" knowledge is power.

Before you step away from this book, I encourage you to journal your responses to the following questions:

- What actions will you take now that you have read and finished this book?
- What life changes will you make?
- What habits will you develop?
- What goals will you set?
- What skills will you develop?
- What relationships will you invest in?
- What seminars and training will you attend?
- Which mentors will you seek?

How will you continue to become the person who can dream big dreams, create, and live those dreams?

COMMIT TO YOU AND YOUR FUTURE

Your life is on the line, and whatever happens next, it is under your control. The advantage is this time, you are starting from higher ground. Commit to yourself to keep going.

In the ten lines below, list out the ten actions you commit to take within the next 90 days because of reading this book.

1. _____
2. _____
3. _____
4. _____
5. _____
6. _____
7. _____
8. _____
9. _____
10. _____

It doesn't stop here! Your next mountain will require you to keep growing to meet its challenges. But don't worry. You have done it once and can do it again. That's the great thing about what you have just learned. It is repeatable.

Now that you have read my book, I encourage you to contact me.
Tell me what you liked and what you didn't so I can improve it for the next edition.
Most importantly, tell me about you, your challenges, your obstacles, and your adversities so I can help you achieve your success.
In fact, I would like to offer you a complimentary, no-obligation consultation by phone or in-person (if geography allows).
My email address is Wendy@WendyMarman.com.
I wish you success and prosperity!
I wish you happy relationships and vibrant health.
I wish you all the success in the world as you have chosen for you.

Wendy Marman

Did you resonate with the message in this book?

If you are wondering…

What's Next?

Visit
https//www.WendyMarman.com
to stay updated on events, workshops, book tour information, etc.

If you would like to connect with Wendy Marman
about coaching services, speaking engagements, or consulting services,
email her at
Wendy@WendyMarman.com

To obtain your own D.I.S.C. Personality Assessment, go to
https://www.personalityservice.com/portal/marm/store

www.ingramcontent.com/pod-product-compliance
Lightning Source LLC
Chambersburg PA
CBHW021425070526
44577CB00001B/66